D0757734

Miguel de Cervantes

Miguel de Cervantes

Jake Goldberg

CHELSEA HOUSE PUBLISHERS
NEW YORK ■ PHILADELPHIA

CHELSEA HOUSE PUBLISHERS

Editorial Director: Richard Rennert
Executive Managing Editor: Karyn Gullen Browne
Executive Editor: Sean Dolan
Copy Chief: Philip Koslow
Picture Editor: Adrian G. Allen
Art Director: Nora Wertz
Manufacturing Director: Gerald Levine
Systems Manager: Lindsey Ottman
Production Coordinator: Marie Claire Cebrián-Ume

HISPANICS OF ACHIEVEMENT
Senior Editor: John W. Selfridge

Staff for *MIGUEL DE CERVANTES*
Copy Editor: Margaret Dornfeld
Designer: Robert Yaffe
Picture Researcher: Wendy P. Wills
Cover Illustration: Daniel O'Leary

5   7   9   8   6   4

Library of Congress Cataloging-in-Publication Data
Jake Goldberg.
Miguel de Cervantes/Jake Goldberg.
p. cm.—(Hispanics of achievement)
Includes bibliographical references and index.
Summary: Describes the life and career of the noted Spanish writer, including
the creation of his masterpiece "Don Quixote."
ISBN 0-7910-1238-7
0-7910-1265-4 (pbk.)
1. Cervantes Saavedra, Miguel de, 1547–1616—Juvenile literature. 2. Authors,
Spanish—17th century—Biography—Juvenile literature. [1. Authors, Spanish.]
I. Title. II. Series.
92-32543
PQ6337.G62 1993
CIP
863'.3—dc20
AC

CONTENTS

JOAN BAEZ
Mexican-American folksinger

RUBÉN BLADES
Panamanian lawyer and entertainer

JORGE LUIS BORGES
Argentine writer

PABLO CASALS
Spanish cellist and conductor

MIGUEL DE CERVANTES
Spanish writer

CESAR CHAVEZ
Mexican-American labor leader

EL CID
Spanish military leader

ROBERTO CLEMENTE
Puerto Rican baseball player

SALVADOR DALÍ
Spanish painter

PLÁCIDO DOMINGO
Spanish singer

GLORIA ESTEFAN
Cuban-American singer

GABRIEL GARCÍA MÁRQUEZ
Colombian writer

PANCHO GONZALES
Mexican-American tennis player

FRANCISCO JOSÉ DE GOYA
Spanish painter

FRIDA KAHLO
Mexican painter

JOSÉ MARTÍ
Cuban revolutionary and poet

RITA MORENO
Puerto Rican singer and actress

PABLO NERUDA
Chilean poet and diplomat

ANTONIA NOVELLO
U.S. surgeon general

OCTAVIO PAZ
Mexican poet and critic

PABLO PICASSO
Spanish artist

ANTHONY QUINN
Mexican-American actor

OSCAR DE LA RENTA
Dominican fashion designer

DIEGO RIVERA
Mexican painter

LINDA RONSTADT
Mexican-American singer

ANTONIO LÓPEZ DE SANTA ANNA
Mexican general and politician

GEORGE SANTAYANA
Spanish philosopher and poet

JUNÍPERO SERRA
Spanish missionary and explorer

LEE TREVINO
Mexican-American golfer

DIEGO VELÁZQUEZ
Spanish painter

PANCHO VILLA
Mexican revolutionary

CHELSEA HOUSE PUBLISHERS

HISPANICS OF ACHIEVEMENT

Rodolfo Cardona

The Spanish language and many other elements of Spanish culture are present in the United States today and have been since
the country's earliest beginnings. Some of these elements have come
directly from the Iberian Peninsula; others have come indirectly, by
way of Mexico, the Caribbean basin, and the countries of Central
and South America.

Spanish culture has influenced America in many subtle ways,
and consequently many Americans remain relatively unaware of
the extent of its impact. The vast majority of them recognize the
influence of Spanish culture in America, but they often do not
realize the great importance and long history of that influence.
This is partly because Americans have tended to judge the
Hispanic influence in the United States in statistical terms rather
than to look closely at the ways in which individual Hispanics
have profoundly affected American culture. For this reason, it is
fitting that Americans obtain more than a passing acquaintance
with the origins of these Spanish cultural elements and gain an
understanding of how they have been woven into the fabric of
American society.

It is well documented that Spanish seafarers were the first to
explore and colonize many of the early territories of what is
today called the United States of America. For this reason, stu-

dents of geography discover Hispanic names all over the map of the United States. For instance, the Strait of Juan de Fuca was named after the Spanish explorer who first navigated the waters of the Pacific Northwest; the names of states such as Arizona (arid zone), Montana (mountain), Florida (thus named because it was reached on Easter Sunday, which in Spanish is called the feast of Pascua Florida), and California (named after a fictitious land in one of the first and probably the most popular among the Spanish novels of chivalry, *Amadis of Gaul*) are all derived from Spanish; and there are numerous mountains, rivers, canyons, towns, and cities with Spanish names throughout the United States.

Not only explorers but many other illustrious figures in Spanish history have helped define American culture. For example, the 13th-century king of Spain, Alfonso X, also known as the Learned, may be unknown to the majority of Americans, but his work on the codification of Spanish law has greatly influenced the evolution of American law, particularly in the jurisdictions of the Southwest. For this contribution a statue of him stands in the rotunda of the Capitol in Washington, D.C. Likewise, the name Diego Rivera may be unfamiliar to most Americans, but this Mexican painter influenced many American artists whose paintings, commissioned during the Great Depression and the New Deal era of the 1930s, adorn the walls of government buildings throughout the United States. In recent years the contributions of Puerto Ricans, Mexicans, Mexican Americans (Chicanos), and Cubans in American cities such as Boston, Chicago, Los Angeles, Miami, Minneapolis, New York, and San Antonio have been enormous.

The importance of the Spanish language in this vast cultural complex cannot be overstated. Spanish, after all, is second only to English as the most widely spoken of Western languages within the United States as well as in the entire world. The popularity of the Spanish language in America has a long history.

In addition to Spanish exploration of the New World, the great Spanish literary tradition served as a vehicle for bringing the language and culture to America. Interest in Spanish literature in America began when English immigrants brought with them translations of Spanish masterpieces of the Golden Age. As early as 1683, private libraries in Philadelphia and Boston contained copies of the first picaresque novel, *Lazarillo de Tormes*, translations of Francisco de Quevedo's *Los Sueños*, and copies of the immortal epic of reality and illusion *Don Quixote*, by the great Spanish writer Miguel de Cervantes. It would not be surprising if Cotton Mather, the arch-Puritan, read *Don Quixote* in its original Spanish, if only to enrich his vocabulary in preparation for his writing *La fe del cristiano en 24 artículos de la Institución de Cristo, enviada a los españoles para que abran sus ojos* (The Christian's Faith in 24 Articles of the Institution of Christ, Sent to the Spaniards to Open Their Eyes), published in Boston in 1699.

Over the years, Spanish authors and their works have had a vast influence on American literature—from Washington Irving, John Steinbeck, and Ernest Hemingway in the novel to Henry Wadsworth Longfellow and Archibald MacLeish in poetry. Such important American writers as James Fenimore Cooper, Edgar Allan Poe, Walt Whitman, Mark Twain, and Herman Melville all owe a sizable debt to the Spanish literary tradition. Some writers, such as Willa Cather and Maxwell Anderson, who explored Spanish themes they came into contact with in the American Southwest and Mexico, were influenced less directly but no less profoundly.

Important contributions to a knowledge of Spanish culture in the United States were also made by many lesser known individuals—teachers, publishers, historians, entrepreneurs, and others—with a love for Spanish culture. One of the most significant of these contributions was made by Abiel Smith, a Harvard College graduate of the class of 1764, when he bequeathed stock worth $20,000 to Harvard for the support of a professor of French and Spanish. By 1819 this endowment had produced enough income to appoint a professor, and the philologist and humanist George Ticknor became the first holder of the Abiel

Smith Chair, which was the very first endowed Chair at Harvard University. Other illustrious holders of the Smith Chair would include the poets Henry Wadsworth Longfellow and James Russell Lowell.

A highly respected teacher and scholar, Ticknor was also a collector of Spanish books, and as such he made a very special contribution to America's knowledge of Spanish culture. He was instrumental in amassing for Harvard libraries one of the first and most impressive collections of Spanish books in the United States. He also had a valuable personal collection of Spanish books and manuscripts, which he bequeathed to the Boston Public Library.

With the creation of the Abiel Smith Chair, Spanish language and literature courses became part of the curriculum at Harvard, which also went on to become the first American university to offer graduate studies in Romance languages. Other colleges and universities throughout the United States gradually followed Harvard's example, and today Spanish language and culture may be studied at most American institutions of higher learning.

No discussion of the Spanish influence in the United States, however brief, would be complete without a mention of the Spanish influence on art. Important American artists such as John Singer Sargent, James A. M. Whistler, Thomas Eakins, and Mary Cassatt all explored Spanish subjects and experimented with Spanish techniques. Virtually every serious American artist living today has studied the work of the Spanish masters as well as the great 20th-century Spanish painters Salvador Dalí, Joan Miró, and Pablo Picasso.

The most pervasive Spanish influence in America, however, has probably been in music. Compositions such as Leonard Bernstein's *West Side Story*, the Latinization of William Shakespeare's *Romeo and Juliet* set in New York's Puerto Rican quarter, and Aaron Copland's *Salon Mexico* are two obvious examples. In general, one can hear the influence of Latin rhythms—from tango to mambo, from guaracha to salsa—in virtually every form of American music.

This series of biographies, which Chelsea House has published under the general title HISPANICS OF ACHIEVEMENT, constitutes further recognition of—and a renewed effort to bring forth to the consciousness of America's young people—the contributions that Hispanic people have made not only in the United States but throughout the civilized world. The men and women who are featured in this series have attained a high level of accomplishment in their respective fields of endeavor and have made a permanent mark on American society.

The title of this series must be understood in its broadest possible sense: The term *Hispanics* is intended to include Spaniards, Spanish Americans, and individuals from many countries whose language and culture have either direct or indirect Spanish origins. The names of many of the people included in this series will be immediately familiar; others will be less recognizable. All, however, have attained recognition within their own countries, and often their fame has transcended their borders.

The series HISPANICS OF ACHIEVEMENT thus addresses the attainments and struggles of Hispanic people in the United States and seeks to tell the stories of individuals whose personal and professional lives in some way reflect the larger Hispanic experience. These stories are exemplary of what human beings can accomplish, often against daunting odds and by extraordinary personal sacrifice, where there is conviction and determination. Fray Junípero Serra, the 18th-century Spanish Franciscan missionary, is one such individual. Although in very poor health, he devoted the last 15 years of his life to the foundation of missions throughout California—then a mostly unsettled expanse of land—in an effort to bring a better life to Native Americans through the cultivation of crafts and animal husbandry. An example from recent times, the Mexican-American labor leader Cesar Chavez has battled bitter opposition and made untold personal sacrifices in his effort to help poor agricultural workers who have been exploited for decades on farms throughout the Southwest.

The talent with which each one of these men and women may have been endowed required dedication and hard work to develop and become fully realized. Many of them have enjoyed rewards for their efforts during their own lifetime, whereas others have died poor and unrecognized. For some it took a long time to achieve their goals, for others success came at an early age, and for still others the struggle continues. All of them, however, stand out as people whose lives have made a difference, whose achievements we need to recognize today and should continue to honor in the future.

Miguel de Cervantes

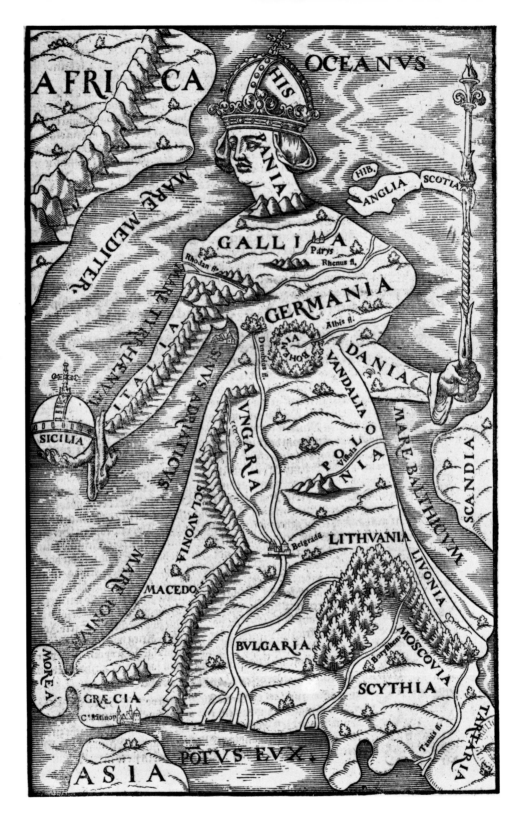

OCTOBER 1597

The old man leaned back against the wall of his cold, damp cell. His bones ached, and when he breathed deeply, he felt a soreness in his chest from the old bullet wounds. The numb fingers of his useless left hand were curled up in a grotesque tangle, the result of another old bullet wound. Sometimes, even now, the hand would start to bleed. But nothing was as disturbing as those bouts of dizziness, that strange unquenchable thirst, that weariness that neither rest nor food could relieve. He knew these were signs of a more profound illness, something the doctors called dropsy, the name they gave to anything they did not understand and could not cure.

He had a long, proud, sorrowful face, a large mustache, a handsome nose, and bright, intelligent eyes. His complexion was pale, and his chestnut hair and golden beard were already quite gray. He wore threadbare and patched clothing. Sometimes when he mumbled something, an old stutter would reassert itself. He asked himself, what was he, a 50-year-old Spanish gentleman, doing in a place like this?

Around him in the large cell, other prisoners shuffled about in the darkness. The place smelled of tobacco, urine, sweat, and alcohol. It was never really quiet. During the day, the corridors swarmed with the

This 16th-century map takes more than a few geographical liberties but is accurate in its depiction of Spain as the "head" of Europe. The age of exploration brought about a period of great prosperity in Spain as Spanish galleons returned from their voyages with riches from the New World.

prisoners' lawyers and relatives. At night, there were the hacking coughs of the sick, even the occasional cry of someone about to be murdered by prison toughs. And there were rumors of plague coming up from the south.

The old man knew his fellow prisoners well. He had lived with them outside the prison walls, in the streets and taverns of Seville. Many were, like himself, ex-soldiers, veterans of the interminable wars against the Turks, the Dutch, the French, the English. Others were dispossessed farmers, their lands taken to pay obscenely high taxes. Still others were unemployed craftsmen or impoverished noblemen. They had all come to the city penniless, and they had drifted into a range of sordid professions. There were beggars, card sharps, pickpockets, confidence tricksters, gamblers, thieves, and outright thugs. He had admired them once. They lived free of the behavior dictated by class or social position. They lacked pretension and could size up a man for what he was really worth in an instant. But now, in prison, they were an ugly bunch, without hope or scruples, and they could be

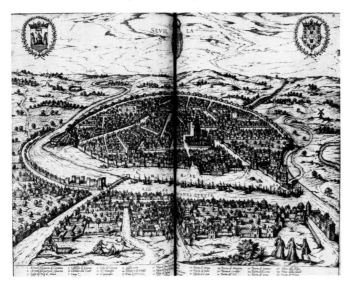

The city of Seville in 1617. During the 16th and 17th centuries— Spain's Golden Age— Spain prospered. Seville, which became the country's most densely populated city, was also Spain's busiest seaport and a thriving artistic and cultural center.

dangerous. This was no way for a gentleman, a war hero, a poet, a devout Catholic, to end up.

Sometimes, when the fatigue and discomfort were severe, his mind would wander back to that other prison, more than 15 years before, in Algiers. The guards were less amenable to bribes then, and they hated his Christian soul. He had been bound in chains then and had witnessed much cruelty. But at that time his companions were prisoners of war, and in spite of the hardships there was a sense of comradeship, of shared purpose, and of heroism in their efforts to stay alive. Here, those same soldiers would steal his purse without a second thought. Here, if a man had a few *reales*, he could have food, wine, or even buy his way out into the streets for the day. Even here, money separated one man from another, and the old man had very little of it. He had never had much money. That was, in fact, why he was in prison.

He had ignored the summons to come to Madrid and explain himself. The king's agents were looking into the accounts of the commissaries, the collectors of grain and provisions for the great fleet that had tried to invade England nine years earlier. The old man had worked for the king, confiscating wheat and other goods from poor farmers and rural gentry alike and keeping precise accounts. He had not stolen anything, but he was accused nonetheless of shorting the government to enrich himself. What nonsense! Where were his riches, then? He had been in the Madrid courts many times to try to straighten this matter out, but they would not let go of it. He refused to go to court again, so they jailed him to make him change his mind.

He should have been thinking about how to explain himself, how to justify his accounts from what records remained in his possession. He should have been thinking about the intricacies of the royal bureaucracy, about how it worked, and who could be flattered or bribed to quietly sweep this business under the rug. Who would champion his cause? Who could be called upon for a loan if things could not be resolved properly? He should have been thinking about all of those things, but he was not.

He was thinking instead about a story he wanted to write in which a superfluous old country gentleman, a man of about his own age, loses his wits and decides to become a knight-errant, a mounted armored soldier of fortune from bygone days of chivalry. This romantic warrior would have incredible adven-

Miguel de Cervantes, the literary genius of Spain's Golden Age, was accused of cheating the government, arrested, and imprisoned in 1597. While in prison he began work on Don Quixote, *a novel that would eventually be acclaimed as one of the great masterpieces of world literature.*

A 16th-century woodcut depicting a reveler. Cervantes is known for the richness of his characters, some of the most memorable of which are based on the humble villagers—barbers, innkeepers, maids, farmers, shopkeepers, vagabonds, revelers, and rogues— whom he met in his travels.

tures as he rode forth to do good deeds and seek justice. He would fail—grandly perhaps, but fail all the same—because his view of the world would be slightly delusional, as were the views of the king, the Church, the Inquisition, and the Spanish nation as a whole, though one dare not say that directly.

The old man could not get the story out of his head. But he would have to get out of prison to put it into writing. Where could he go? Where could he get the peace and quiet to save his waning strength and write? There was his wife's small house in the village of Esquivias—a good place to be if the plague came back. But he had left her after less than a year of marriage. He hardly knew her. If she were charitable enough, after all his restless wandering, she might take him back. It was worth going to see her. In such a quiet country atmosphere, the story would solidify in his mind. He knew he could write it. It was a risk, mainly because it would offend the critics and the clique surrounding Lope de Vega, who had trashed the old man's plays years before. But he felt there was no choice. The story had become so tangible in his mind that it had to be born, and once he was out of jail, he would be able to write it.

CHAPTER

TWO

CERVANTES' SPAIN

W hen English-speaking peoples consider the European Renaissance—the revival of science, art, and commerce during the 15th and 16th centuries following the collapse of the Roman Empire and the ensuing feudal period—they may know something of the great Italian city-states, with their artists and merchant-princes, or something of the prosperous, free-thinking towns of northern Europe. They might focus their attention on the English Renaissance and the reign of the Tudor sovereigns—the age of Queen Elizabeth I and the great dramatist William Shakespeare. Because of language and cultural barriers, however, few would be as well aware of the equally great revival in literature, art, exploration, and conquest that was occurring in Spain at the same time.

The Spanish Renaissance was unique in that it was almost smothered by religious intolerance, and political forces would strangle its growth while new thinking took hold everywhere else in Europe. Nevertheless, it was a remarkable period. This was the age of Columbus and Magellan, the age of Lope de Vega, the age of Miguel de Cervantes. This was Spain's Golden Age.

The Romans invaded Spain in 206 B.C. and ruled for four centuries. They brought Roman law and the

In 1480, King Ferdinand and Queen Isabella established a religious court, the Inquisition, the purpose of which was to ferret out heresy. They formed a police force, the Holy Brotherhood, and assigned it the task of wiping out antimonarchist and non-Christian elements in Spain.

21

Latin language, from which the Spanish language evolved. They also brought the Christian religion. As the Roman Empire disintegrated, various Germanic tribes spread across Europe, and in A.D. 414 the Visigoths overran Spain. The Visigoths, also Christians, ruled over the indigenous people as a loosely knit class of warrior-aristocrats, their kings and princes squabbling with each other and expending their resources in bloody feuds and wars.

Early in the 8th century, Spain was invaded by the Moors, who poured across the Strait of Gibraltar from North Africa. They were not a single group or nation but a confederation of Arabs, Berbers, and Syrians united by their Muslim faith, under the loose control of the sultans of the Ottoman Empire. In A.D. 711 they defeated the last Visigothic king, Roderick, and in successive waves they rapidly took control of the country, to be stopped at the border with France by the armies of Charles Martel in A.D. 732. With some exceptions, the Moors were generally tolerant of the Christians, as well as the large number of Spanish Jews, also immigrants from North Africa. Moorish civilization was economically prosperous and culturally liberal. The cultivation of new crops—oranges, rice, sugarcane, and cotton—was introduced. Christian, Jewish, and Arabic cultures and religions existed side by side and blended with each other, along with Greek philosophy and Persian art. The Moors brought with them extensive knowledge of mathematics, medicine, astronomy, and more advanced agricultural techniques. While the rest of Europe languished in the Dark Ages, the cities of Córdoba, Seville, and Granada became vast, bustling metropolises with huge mosques and fortified palaces known as *alcázars*. Some of their architectural achievements still stand—the Grand Mosque at Córdoba, the Giralda minaret in

Seville, and the grand palace of the Moorish rulers, the Alhambra, in Granada.

Different Moorish groups ruled Spain for almost 800 years, although they were often at war with each other and continuously at war with the remnants of the Christian kingdoms to the north. Indeed, from the Christian point of view the 800-year period was known as the Reconquest, during which time the battle lines between Arab and Christian forces see-sawed back and forth and the Moors were gradually driven back into southern Spain. In 1085 the Christian king Alfonso VI retook the city of Toledo. In 1094 the great knight El Cid, who fought both for and against the Christians in the fragmented politics of the time, recaptured Valencia. The medieval epic *The Poem of the Cid* celebrates his achievements and those of the brotherhood of the knights who fought for king and Christ. Ferdinand III retook Córdoba in 1236 and Seville in 1248.

In 1469, Princess Isabella of Castile married King Ferdinand of Aragon. When Isabella became queen of Castile in 1474, the two kingdoms were united, and the modern nation-state of Spain was created. In 1492, Ferdinand and Isabella retook Granada and moved into the Alhambra, the palace of their Moorish enemies. Less tolerant than the Moorish rulers, however, they expelled the Jews from Spain. In 1502 they demanded that all Muslims either convert to the Christian faith or emigrate. Spain was now, on the surface at least, a unified political and religious entity.

Serving as a religious battleground for eight centuries had a profound effect on Spain's culture and history. For instance, Christian Spain absorbed elements of Moorish art, literature, music, language, architecture, and, through intermarriage, even the physical characteristics of the peoples of North Africa.

At the same time that it absorbed these elements, Christian Spain tried to fight off the Muslim influence. Mosques were torn down and cathedrals built in their place. The Christians took from the Moors their religious zeal and their concept of holy war, and created in Spain a uniquely passionate Catholicism and the concept of the militant religious warrior, expressed in such organizations as the Knights Templars and the Jesuit Order, founded by Ignatius of Loyola in 1539. In 1480, Ferdinand and Isabella established the Inquisition, a religious court intent on ferreting out heresy. No remaining Jew or Muslim, Christian convert or not, was safe from persecution. This was one of the great contradictions of Spanish history—its assimilation of Arabic culture at the same time that it fought with great savagery to free itself from the infidel.

During the Reconquest, Spain's principal source of income was from the sale of wool to the burgeon-

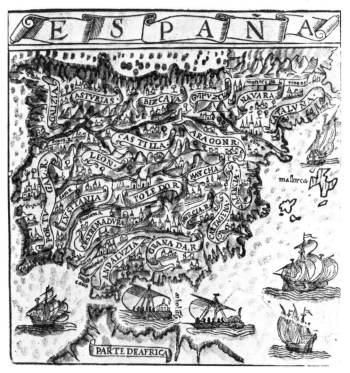

A map showing the provinces of Spain. In 1492, Ferdinand and Isabella sponsored a voyage led by the explorer Christopher Columbus. Their patronage established a lasting cultural and economic link between Europe and the New World.

ing textile industry in Flanders. The Christian kings taxed this income to raise money to finance their wars against the Moors. The need for more and more money put Spain in competition with the Dutch and the Portuguese to find new trade routes to acquire the riches of the East, known to the Europeans since Marco Polo returned from China in 1295. In 1492, Ferdinand and Isabella financed the voyage of Christopher Columbus. Though Columbus never got as far as China, the bounty of the Americas was more than adequate compensation.

In 1516, Charles I ascended the throne, and Spain's aggressive exploration and conquest of the New World began in earnest. In 1520, Ferdinand Magellan sailed west around Cape Horn at the southern tip of South America and later discovered the Philippines. His surviving crew members struggled across the Pacific and Indian oceans, around Cape Horn at the southern tip of Africa, and returned to Spain as the first Europeans to circumnavigate the globe. In 1522, Hernán Cortés conquered the Aztec empire in Mexico with a force of only 1,500 men. In 1534, Francisco Pizarro completed his conquest of the Incas in Peru with only 400 men. These conquistadores (conquerors) not only added vast new territories to the Spanish empire but reinforced the mythology of knight-errantry, of the romantic soldier of fortune whose heroic exploits would earn him fame, adventure, wealth, and a secure place in heaven.

Fame and salvation were all to the good, but it was the wealth of the New World that created Renaissance Spain. The Indian empires of Central and South America were broken up. Their people were enslaved and forced to work on the plantations and in the mines established by the Spanish colonists. Feudal systems of land ownership were transplanted to the Americas, with natives required to provide so many days of free labor to their Spanish lords. The mines

were extremely valuable. During one good year, Spanish galleons might return to the mother country 10,000 pounds of gold and a half million pounds of silver. With this fortune the Spanish paid for their religious wars and a lavish royal court, built palaces and cathedrals, and created a small but wealthy class of people with a taste for literature, art, theater, and other entertainments.

The expansion of world trade that followed the age of exploration, along with the vast wealth that flowed into Europe through Spain, transformed European society, creating the basis for modern capitalism. Relations between people began to be dominated by the payment of money for services rather than by old feudal obligations. Eventually, Europe entered a long period of inflation, the price of labor rose, and land could be had cheaply. People began to see opportunities for advancement.

World trade also required a new type of individual, the entrepreneur. In feudal times, craftsmen produced their wares for local markets, knew their customers, and completed transactions simply and quickly. Now goods arrived from faraway places, had to be paid for in advance, and had to be stored for various periods before final distribution and sale. Large amounts of capital were needed to finance such trade, loans and interest rates became important, and knowledge of foreign currencies, exchange rates, commodity prices, and conditions in foreign markets became essential. Merchants and bankers appeared and became a powerful force throughout Europe, further stimulating trade and manufacture through their investments. Kings became dependent on these bankers and capitalists for loans to build their administrative apparatuses and to fight their wars. The first mass production to occur in Europe was organized by these new capitalists to provide national armies with weapons, ammunition, clothing, and provisions. There were few true factories at this time, but entrepreneurs farmed out work to hundreds and even thousands of small craftsmen in a cottage industry system whereby people in rural areas worked in their homes with

Sixteenth-century women work with wool at a loom. Before the consolidation of workers in factories, rural cottage industries, where people worked at home with tools and raw materials provided by entrepreneurs, thrived throughout Europe.

tools and raw materials supplied by the entrepreneur. Building factories in the towns and cities would not have been practical yet, because the labor force was small and rigidly controlled by the medieval guilds, and there was as yet no understanding of the technology and the power sources that could bring many workers together in one place.

The kings in turn developed policies that protected their manufacturers and traders by encouraging exports and restricting imports of everything but essential raw materials. State-supported trading associations were given special privileges and royal monopolies to control commerce in various areas of the world. But the Spanish sovereigns spent liberally and taxed their own industries so heavily that they collapsed.

At the very time that Charles I was consolidating the Spanish nation with American gold and Catholic doctrine, the rest of Europe was in a state of religious disintegration. The Catholic church had become a wealthy, secular institution, with large holdings in land and an extensive clerical bureaucracy. Its clergy were seen by many to be guilty of personal enrichment, neglect of religious duties, idleness, and corruption, and its popes had become masters of political intrigue. Questions arose about the infallibility of church doctrine, and new religions appeared that claimed one could be saved without the intervention of priests or the fees they demanded. In the 1520s, Lutheranism challenged the authority of the pope in northern Europe. In the 1530s, Calvinism appeared in France. Collectively, these new religious movements were known as the Reformation.

In 1519, Charles I of Spain had assumed the additional title of the Holy Roman Emperor Charles V, heading a loose, fragile alliance of states professing allegiance to the Church of Rome. As a result of his

Spain's king Philip II succeeded his father, Charles I (Charles V of the Holy Roman Empire), in 1556. In an effort to put Europe under the yoke of a single religion, Catholicism, Philip II squandered his country's resources on crusades against the Protestants and Turks.

election, he assumed control over a large area of European territory—including the Netherlands, Burgundy, Luxembourg, the German states of Saxony, Bavaria, Brandenburg, and Silesia, and the Italian states of Naples, Sicily, and Sardinia—and faced the difficult task of maintaining political, economic, and religious control over a large and restless community of kingdoms and principalities. For these states and others, the issue of choosing their religion was closely tied to the issue of how much independence they had from Charles and the papacy. Preservation of the Spanish Empire therefore became linked to the struggle for religious orthodoxy.

Charles I abdicated his throne in 1556 and was succeeded by his son, Philip II, who ruled until his death in 1598. Philip became the symbol of the Counter-Reformation, the movement of a reformed, religiously reinvigorated, and less ostentatious Catholic church to win back Europe from the Protestant dissenters. He established Madrid as the capital of the nation and built a new royal residence, the Escorial, about 30 miles outside the city. From there he plotted to make Europe once again an empire with one religion, becoming so obsessed with this goal that he neglected his own country's well-being, spending

In 1561, Philip II moved the Spanish capital to Madrid and, a few years later, began construction on the Escorial, an enormous palace about 30 miles northwest of the city. It took more than 20 years and the labor of 300 men working day and night to complete the construction project.

its resources on crusades against the Protestants and the Turks, who threatened Europe from the east.

Despite the squandering of Spain's resources in foreign wars and the suffocating religious orthodoxy, the arts flourished in Spain as they never had before. The Golden Age produced three great painters: Doménikos Theotokópoulos, or El Greco (the Greek), Diego Velázquez, and Bartolomé Esteban Murillo. All three painters, in their portraits of kings, popes, and important personages, reveal that in spite of attempts by religious authorities to isolate Spain from the heresies of Europe, artists were able to absorb the fundamental principle of Renaissance humanism— that the depiction of the strengths and weaknesses of human character was more important than the depiction of position, wealth, or power.

In literature, the Golden Age began with the poetry of Garcilaso de la Vega, who created visions of medieval romance in pastoral settings. Other literary artists of the period include the poet Santa Teresa; Luis de Góngora, the bard of Córdoba; the actor and playwright Lope de Rueda; and the most prolific, and next to Cervantes the greatest, literary figure of the Golden Age, Félix Lope de Vega. The author of more than 500 plays, Lope de Vega helped establish a national theater in Spain. The last great dramatist of the period was Calderón de la Barca, whose plays had strong Catholic themes. The Golden Age also saw a vast outpouring of folk music, romantic ballads, lyric poetry, music for the Spanish guitar, and baroque architecture.

But the cultural achievements of Spain's Golden Age were tarnished as Spain tried desperately to keep the Holy Roman Empire intact and Catholic by waging war against France, the Netherlands, England, the Turkish empire, and even against some of the popes, whom the Spanish kings regarded as inferior

During his lifetime, the Spanish dramatist Félix Lope de Vega was idolized by nobles and commoners alike. The author of more than 500 plays, Lope de Vega was instrumental in the development of a national theater in Spain during the 16th century.

to themselves in the Catholic heirarchy. Although Charles I was equally responsible, it was during Philip II's reign that the cost of endless foreign wars began to exhaust the treasury. Eventually, Philip was spending almost 70 percent of his earnings to service his debts. As king, he was entitled to a fifth of the wealth brought back by the treasure galleons, but increasingly the treasure was transferred directly and entirely from the holds of the galleons to Philip's creditors.

The wars also drained Spain of its most talented and energetic young men. Royal taxations and lack of domestic investment brought about stagnation and poverty, filling the streets of Spanish cities with a new class of *pícaros*: beggars, vagabonds, derelicts, thieves, con men, unemployed soldiers, and impoverished noblemen with nothing to show for themselves but their war records. They became the material for a new type of Spanish literature, the picaresque novel, usually in the form of an earthy, episodic account of the adventures of some down-and-out rogue or conniver who knew his way around the seamier side of Spanish society. One such novel, *La atalaya de la vida humana, aventuras y vida del pícaro Guzmán de Alfarache* (The Panorama of Human Life, Adventures and Life of the Rogue Guzmán de Alfarache), written by Mateo Alemán, greatly influenced Cervantes' work. Spanish public life, with its gambling halls and brothels, its bloody bullfights, and its public hangings and burnings of heretics, took on qualities of immoderation and brutality.

As the wars continued, religious fervor and royal egotism began to cloud Philip's mind. Two events during his reign—critical events in the life of Cervantes as well—signaled the Spanish decline. In 1571, Spanish forces fought and won a great naval battle, defeating the Turks at Lepanto off the coast of Greece. But the victory was never exploited, and the threat of Turkish westward expansion was not checked. Two years after Lepanto, the Turks returned and seized the Spanish outpost at Tunis, and Spanish ships in the Mediterranean remained at risk from piratical attacks by the Barbary States of North Africa. Lepanto became a hollow victory and created a bitter feeling in the minds of many war veterans who, like Cervantes, suffered greatly in its aftermath. In 1588, Spanish fantasies collapsed with the total defeat of the "invincible" Armada by an English navy under the command of Lord Howard of Effingham, exposing the ineptness of the country's political and military administration.

These events fatigued the Spanish nation, eroding its pride and casting doubt on the grandiose sense of mission of El Cid, of Ferdinand and Isabella, of Columbus and Magellan, of Cortés, Pizarro, and the conquistadores, of all those who had died in foreign lands in the cause of Christ, and of the whole tradition of Spanish knight-errantry itself. In this climate of broken dreams, it was possible for an aging, worldly-wise former soldier to write an affectionate yet biting parody of a Spanish nobleman who was so pompously incompetent that he had to be protected from himself by his shrewd peasant companion.

This was *Don Quixote*, the greatest work of Spanish literature and one of the greatest novels of all time. Its author, Miguel de Cervantes Saavedra, was an impoverished gentleman, a wounded veteran of a ferocious naval battle, and a captive of an eastern potentate, from whose pestilential Algerian prison he had tried to escape four times. He was a vagabond, a tax collector, and a supplier of food and provisions for the Spanish Armada. As a poet and playwright he was a humanist, a realist, and a satirist of the pretensions of his age. A passionate Catholic and a faithful supporter of his king, he remained a man of faith and optimism, and his fame has outlasted that of kings and popes.

DONPHILIPPE

YOUTH

T he exact date of birth of Miguel de Cervantes is
not known, but it was certainly no more than a
few days before his baptism in the church of Santa
María la Mayor, in the small city of Alcalá de Henares
20 miles northwest of Madrid, on October 9, 1547.
His family lived at 2 Calle de la Imagen, a street in a
quarter of the city heavily settled by *Maranos* and
Moriscos, Jews and Muslims who had embraced Chris-
tianity, officially at least, rather than face expulsion
from Spain. The city of Alcalá de Henares was known
mainly for its university, founded in 1508 by the
infamous Cardinal Jiménez de Cisneros, who during
the reign of Ferdinand and Isabella had held public
book burnings of Arabic religious literature. The
university became a center for liberal and humanist
thought. The writer Francisco de Quevedo and the
playwright Félix Lope de Vega would be students
there. But its first chancellor, Pedro de Lerma, a friend
of Erasmus's, was imprisoned and eventually hounded
out of the country by the Inquisition. Such were the
obstacles strewn in the path of Spanish Renaissance
scholarship.

The year of Cervantes' birth was an eventful one
in European history. Spain was still a wealthy and
powerful country, but the signs of decay and bank-

ruptcy were also apparent. Charles I was still on the throne, and had in fact just won a great victory over Protestant forces at the battle of Mühlberg in Germany. But he had put the monarchy deeply into debt to do it. In 1547, Henry VIII of England died, initiating the final struggle between the Catholic Mary and the Protestant Elizabeth for the religious destiny of the kingdom. The heretic Martin Luther had died the year before, but his ideas were still spreading throughout Europe. The conquistador Hernán Cortés died that year. Ivan the Terrible became czar of Russia. And in 1547 the Church of Rome issued its first *Index* of prohibited books, which included all the Bibles translated into the vernacular, that is, languages other than the officially recognized Latin, as well as the works of Erasmus.

Desiderius Erasmus of Rotterdam, who lived from about 1466 to 1536, was a humanist scholar and writer and a central figure of the Renaissance. He translated, and in effect revived, the works of Aristotle, Cicero, Ovid, Plutarch, Suetonius, Seneca, and other classical Greek and Roman writers. In his own *In Praise of Folly* and other works, he satirized the abuses of the Church, becoming immensely popular throughout Europe and in Spain as well. But he never sided with the Lutherans in calling for armed rebellion, and he remained a loyal if troublesome Catholic all his life. The banning of his books reflected the inflexible and humorless way the Church would respond to perceived heresy. But his ideas could not be erased so easily, and many of Cervantes' early teachers were of Erasmus's more liberal Catholic persuasion. At the time of his birth, Miguel was the youngest of three children. A first son, Andrés, had died. Miguel had two living sisters, Luisa, born the year before, and three-year-old Andrea. His mother, Doña Leonor de Cortinas, was the daughter of small landowners in nearby Arganda. His father, Rodrigo de Cervantes, was a surgeon, but a surgeon in 16th-century Spain was closer to a barber or a butcher than a doctor. He could lance boils, set broken bones, pull teeth, and stitch up minor wounds, but that was about the extent of his expertise. It might be argued that the professional physicians of the time had little medical knowledge beyond this; but whereas a doctor might serve the high nobility, a surgeon was more likely to attend to the victims of a street brawl, and for this reason poverty dogged the Cervantes family throughout Miguel's youth. Miguel's great-grandfather, Ruy de Cervantes, had been a successful cloth merchant, and his grandfather, Juan de Cervantes, was a lawyer who worked for the Inquisition and who had acquired a small fortune under suspicious circumstances. But none of the wealth or property acquired by the family was shared with Miguel's father, who was looked upon as an incompetent provider.

The record of Miguel's early life is sketchy. In 1550, his younger brother Rodrigo was born. Unable to eke out a living from his meager surgeon's fees and accused of incompetence by one of his patients, in 1551 Miguel's father took the family north to the city of Valladolid in an effort to make a fresh start. Valladolid was the location of the royal court, though at the time Spain had no official capital city, and the king was likely to be away somewhere leading his armies. But the city was prosperous, and the Cervantes family had hopes. In 1552, another child, Magdalena, was born, and all these mouths to feed increased the burden on the hapless father. Unable to pay his rent, he was thrown into debtor's prison.

By custom, a *hidalgo*, a gentleman in the old sense of the word as a person of noble birth, one who held even some minor title and could distinguish himself from the commoners, could not be imprisoned for debt. Rodrigo de Cervantes attempted to prove that he was a lesser member of the gentry. It is not clear that the claim was well supported, but for the rest of his life Miguel de Cervantes would claim status as minor nobility. In any case, the father was released from prison in 1553. Still penniless, the family returned briefly to Alcalá de Henares, and then moved again to try their fortunes in Córdoba, far to the south on the Guadalquivir River. In 1555, another brother, Juan, was born. For a number of years after 1557, there is no record at all of the Cervantes family. They may have been on the move again, or Rodrigo may have simply been lucky enough to stay out of debt for a while—most of the records concerning him at this time are IOUs and legal petitions for payment from his creditors. It was also a time of drought, famine, and plague in Spain, and the histories of many families were undoubtedly disrupted. The family reappeared in the city of Seville in 1564, when Miguel was 17 years old.

Situated on the Guadalquivir just a short distance from where the river joins the Atlantic Ocean, Seville was Spain's most important seaport. It was a large, busy, prosperous commercial center, where ships from all over the known world unloaded their cargos. Every spring, vessels were loaded with goods for the colonists of the New World, and every fall the treasure galleons would return with their heavy loads of gold and silver. The streets were filled with merchants, traders, and sailors from all over Europe, and the atmosphere was cosmopolitan.

Little is known about Cervantes' early formal schooling. He may or may not have briefly attended one of the new Jesuit academies either here in Seville or earlier in Córdoba. He knew Latin and the classics, but he never absorbed the strict Catholicism the Jesuits would have taught him. Certainly the streets of Seville presented him with a rich education of another kind. Being poor, he undoubtedly mingled with the city's pícaros and learned to see the greatness of the Spanish empire from its underside. His revulsion for the excesses of the Inquisition may have come from watching one of the city's public execution of heretics. Lope de Rueda, the goldsmith turned actor and playwright, was in Seville in 1564 with his traveling players, and it seems likely that Cervantes attended performances.

In 1564, Cervantes' elder sister Andrea met Nicolas de Ovando, became pregnant, and gave birth to an illegitimate daughter the following year. The young man refused to marry her, and Andrea demanded compensation. It was a typical case of promises made and broken by a spoiled, young aristocrat, but it set the pattern for the beautiful Andrea's many romances and flirtations. The younger Magdalena would follow in Andrea's footsteps. His sister Luisa, on the other hand, decided to become a Carmelite nun, and in 1564, Cervantes, in the company of his father, traveled back to Alcalá de Henares to watch her take her vows. On their way back to Seville, they passed through Córdoba just in time to witness the elaborate funeral of Lope de Rueda, who had been performing in Seville earlier in the year.

It was not long before the elder Cervantes was in debt again, and in 1566 the family moved to Madrid in yet another effort to start over. Philip II had been on the throne for 10 years, following the abdication of his father in 1556, and Philip had decided to make Madrid the permanent royal capital of the country. Tens of thousands of court officials, their families, and attendants swarmed into the new capital, swelling its population to five times what it had been just a few years before.

Rodrigo de Cervantes hoped to build a new clientele for his simple surgeon's skills. Thanks to the generosity of Gian Francesco Locadelo, an Italian merchant banker who boarded with the Cervanteses and took a fancy to the flirtatious Andrea, the family enjoyed a few years of modest prosperity. For the first time, a record exists of Miguel's enrollment in school. At the age of 19, he attended the Estudio de la Villa, a city-financed public school run by Juan López de Hoyas, a local parish priest with sympathy for the humanist teachings of Erasmus.

However, the mood at Philip's court was dark and merciless, and the king's narrow, uncompromising militancy was about to cause trouble for Spain. First, he intensified the persecution of the Moriscos, the converted Moors. It was no longer enough to be Christian. They were now forbidden from speaking or writing in Arabic, using their Arabic names, or wearing Moorish clothing.

In the year that the Cervantes family moved to Madrid, 200 nobles of the 17 provinces of the Spanish Netherlands formed a league and petitioned Philip to keep the Inquisition out of their territory. Philip refused, and in August of 1566 angry mobs looted and destroyed Catholic churches in Antwerp, Amsterdam, Utrecht, Leyden, and Delft. Philip responded by sending the duke of Alba with an army of 20,000 soldiers to crush the rebellion. In 1567, Philip's forces had taken captive three prominent rebellious noblemen, Count Egmond, Count Horn, and Baron de Montigny. A less rigid personality might have seen the potential for negotiation, but Philip had all three men executed. The courts of the Inquisition that followed the duke of Alba's troops executed thousands more,

Spanish soldiers commit atrocities in the Netherlands in the name of the Inquisition. When 200 nobles in the Spanish Netherlands signed a petition and formed a league in an effort to resist the Inquisition, Philip sent an army of 20,000 to thwart the resistance.

uniting all resistance against the Spanish occupation and committing Spain to a long, expensive, and bloody war.

In 1566, Suleiman the Magnificent, sultan of the Ottoman Empire, died, leaving the throne to his son, Selim II. The Turks, ruling from Constantinople, controlled a vast area stretching from southern Russia through the Middle East to North Africa. They had pushed and probed across the Mediterranean for 50 years, threatening the lucrative shipping routes of Spain and the Italian city-states. When Turkish military pressure increased under the new sultan, both Pope Pius V and the city of Venice petitioned Philip II for a new offensive to throw back the Muslims and protect commerce. Spain was now moving toward war on two fronts, northern Europe and the Mediterranean.

What manner of man was the young Miguel de Cervantes as these events were unfolding? He had been raised in an atmosphere of genteel poverty, and he had called many places home. He knew the rough and colorful street life of Spain's great cities. He had some education, but no skill or profession. Having some pretensions to the title of hidalgo, he would have shunned a career as a worker or tradesman. His father's failure would have pushed him in other directions in any case. He watched as ambitious friends rose to become part of the royal or ecclesiastical hierarchy, but for Cervantes no opportunities presented themselves. Some biographers have suggested that he was stigmatized by some distant Jewish ancestry, that he came from a family of converted Jews who would not have been fully trusted. True or not, the court was closed to him, and he was temperamentally unsuited for the Church, which had become a huge, parasitic institution employing one out of every five Spaniards. He tried his hand at poetry, and in 1568 his elegy on the death of Philip's young queen, Elizabeth of Valois, was published.

Perhaps he dreamed of the knights and conquistadores of Spain's romantic past, and compared their world to the squalor and harshness he saw about him. Perhaps he was something of a proud and hotheaded

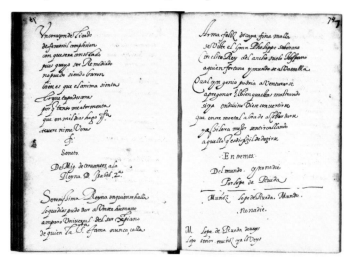

The manuscript of Cervantes' earliest known work, a sonnet written to Queen Elizabeth of Valois. It is believed that Cervantes wrote the poem on the occasion of the birth of the queen's second daughter, Princess Catalina Micaela, on October 10, 1567.

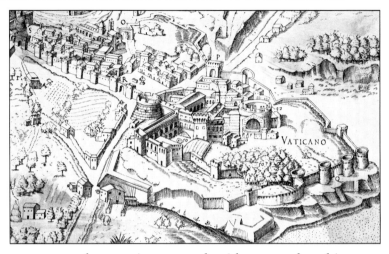

The Vatican, in Rome, Italy, houses the administrative authority of the Catholic church. On September 15, 1569, fleeing a warrant for his arrest, Cervantes left Spain and took refuge in Rome, where in 1570 he found employment as a chamberlain at the Vatican.

young tough, strutting around with a sword at his waist. This is suggested by his involvement in a duel and his wounding of a certain Antonio de Sigura. The details are not clear, but on September 15, 1569, the king's agents issued a warrant for the arrest of Cervantes, specifying as punishment the removal of his right hand and 10 years exile. Cervantes did not wait around to be arrested. At the age of 22, he left Madrid and quickly thereafter left Spain altogether. He took refuge in Rome and in 1570 found employment as a chamberlain, one of a number of butler-secretaries, to Cardinal Giulio Acquaviva. It was a fairly menial position, but it put him inside the world of the Vatican. From this vantage point, all the intrigues and maneuvers of European, indeed, of world politics, were revealed to him.

The Turkish threat was the gravest concern at the moment. The Turks had invaded the island of Cyprus, one of the easternmost outposts of Christian Europe, and were methodically besieging and destroying one Christian garrison after another. The Venetians, with great wealth but not much military power, were frantically demanding the protection of a Spanish army while secretly negotiating with the Turks for a separate peace. But Selim II was also wielding a double-edged sword. In May 1571, in the midst of talks, the Venetians were astounded to learn that a new force of 100 galleys had been sent to strengthen the Turkish fleet at Cyprus. Selim's negotiations were a sham. Though they distrusted each other, it did not take long for the Spaniards and the Italians to conclude a military alliance and begin preparations for war. Philip put the Spanish fleet and army under the command of Don Juan de Austria, whom he openly distrusted for being as impetuous as he himself was cautious.

Suffocated by his role as servant to the servant of Pope Pius V—a man as grim and fanatical as Philip II—having no other prospects, perhaps caught up in

Don Juan de Austria, Philip II's illegitimate half brother, led the powerful Spanish, Roman, and Venetian fleet of 200 ships against the Turks at the Battle of Lepanto. Some 30,000 Turks died at Lepanto, and 7,000 were taken prisoner; of the 28,000 Spanish infantry at Lepanto, more than 7,000 died and 15,000 were wounded.

the clamor for a Christian crusade against the infidel, or perhaps in search of a measure of adventure due him as a descendant of knights and conquistadores, Cervantes left Rome for Naples. There a Spanish army was massing for a thrust at the Turks, and among them was Miguel's younger brother Rodrigo, a new recruit to the company commanded by Diego de Urbina, a unit of the *tercio*, a regiment of about 3,000 men commanded by Miguel de Mencado. Cervantes enlisted in the Spanish infantry, joining his brother's company, and together they surrendered themselves to the fortunes of war.

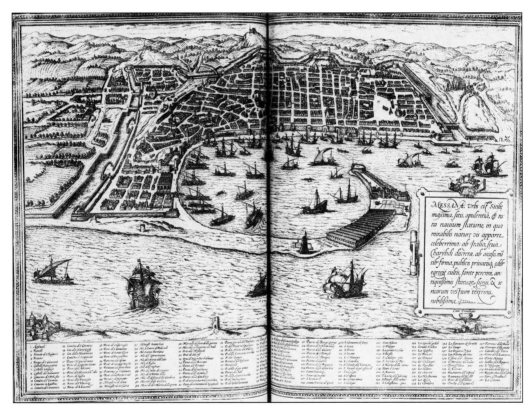

Messina, the Sicilian port to which the Christian fleet retreated following the Battle of Lepanto. Cervantes fought in the battle, was seriously wounded, and was hospitalized at Messina.

GLORY

In August 1571, Cervantes had barely three weeks in which to learn his new trade of soldiering. He was an ordinary infantryman, and his weapon was the *harquebus*, a long, heavy musket. It was difficult to load and hopelessly inaccurate beyond 100 yards. It was looked down upon by other soldiers, who thought their swords and pikes were the weapons of brave men and the harquebus the weapon of an assassin. Yet at close range, a massed volley from even this kind of primitive firearm could cut down a whole line of the enemy. Its heavy ball had a tendency to disintegrate when the weapon was discharged, making the harquebus an unwieldy but deadly shotgun. Cervantes' main concern, however, would have been going through the complex loading drill correctly so that the weapon would not blow up in his face.

Cervantes' company probably consisted of about 250 men. A dozen or more companies formed a *tercio*. The recruiting drives in Spain were thorough, and many of Cervantes' friends and relatives were soldiers too. The army was notorious for its ill-disciplined and riotous behavior, and many residents of Naples were anxious to see them leave. Cervantes himself loved to gamble and enjoyed himself as much as anyone in the rough company of his comrades. With their shiny steel helmets, their bright red shirts, and colorful sashes and trimmings, the Spanish troops were known as *papagayos*, (parrots). In late August, the ranks of Spanish infantry filed through the streets of Naples and down to the docks, where they packed themselves into the galleys of Don Juan de Austria's battle fleet. Miguel and Rodrigo were assigned to the *Marquesa*, commanded by Captain Francisco de Sancto Pietro. Philip had to lend ships and troops to allies who lacked sufficient forces, so the *Marquesa* would sail with the Venetian squadrons under the command of Sebastian Veniero.

There were more than 300 ships in the fleet of the Holy League, as the Christians styled themselves, about 250 of them the standard Mediterranean man-of-war, the galley. The galley varied from 120 to 170 feet in length, but was only 15 to 20 feet wide. It had a displacement of about 170 tons. At its bow it had a

Spanish galleons. Galley warfare during the 16th century was a bloody affair in which ships would ram each other and infantry would storm the decks of enemy vessels in an effort to take possession of them. Severely gored galleons were pillaged and burned; the enemy forces were usually left to drown.

Sixteenth-century Spanish infantrymen usually wore metal breastplates and helmets for close, hand-to-hand fighting. At Lepanto, Cervantes wore the colorful, so-called parrot uniform (center), which allowed for greater freedom of movement but afforded little protection.

bronze-covered battering ram. Some ships had two masts with lateen, or triangular, sails, so that they could tack, or sail against the wind. Without sails, the galley could still make more than six knots, or about seven miles per hour, when rowed. Each vessel had between 30 and 40 oars, each manned by three to six men. The rowers were mostly convicts and slaves, who led a miserable existence. Conditions were not much better for the sailors and supporting infantry, crowded into tight, unsanitary quarters infested with fleas, lice, and rats. Altogether the fleet mounted 1,800 cannon and carried 80,000 men, about 28,000 of them Spanish infantry.

The fleet left Naples and on August 25 reached Messina on the island of Sicily. Here the Christian forces waited three weeks while Don Juan de Austria struggled to bring his ships up to fighting trim and to keep Spanish and Italian commanders from arguing over who was in charge. In the near tropical climate of the Mediterranean summer, Cervantes was stricken with malaria and spent those weeks shivering and sweating below deck, nursed by his brother Rodrigo.

Finally, on September 16, the fleet left Messina and reached the island of Corfu on September 27. Cautiously moving down the western coast of Greece, the ships anchored off Cephalonia on October 4. Here it was learned that the last garrison on Cyprus at Famagusta had surrendered back in early August. The survivors had either been slaughtered or marched off into slavery. This news galvanized the Christian forces, and petty rivalries were forgotten. The Turkish fleet, under the command of Ali Pasha, was probably somewhere near Crete by this time, just on the other side of the Peloponnesian peninsula. Slowly the fleet

The Battle of Lepanto, which Cervantes called the "noblest occasion that centuries past have seen and those to come can hope to see." Cervantes, who was wounded three times in the battle and lost the use of his left arm, spent six months in the hospital recovering.

moved eastward, probing into the Gulf of Corinth, which separates the Pelopennisos from mainland Greece. They approached the narrow straight at Lepanto, now known as Návpaktos, but did not enter because Turkish artillery was positioned on both shores. On October 7, 1571, the masts of the Turkish fleet were sighted about 15 miles away, moving west through the narrow channel, their pennants and banners displayed for battle.

On the *Marquesa*, drums and trumpets sounded the alarm, and Cervantes, still weak and feverish, struggled on deck with his company. His comrades, his brother, and even the captain urged him to go below, telling him he was too sick to fight. Cervantes refused and was finally assigned a position amidships.

The two navies formed two irregular north-south lines, the Turks coming on from the east, the Christians from the west. The narrowness of the channel prevented much maneuvering. Ali Pasha also had 300 ships and at least as many sailors and soldiers as the Holy League. But his spies had miscounted, and the Turkish admiral believed he had numerical superiority. A Spanish reserve of 50 ships had gone undetected. Furthermore, the Spanish had six *galleasses*, hulking, oversized galleys with 50 cannons and a complement of 300 harquebusiers each. As the two fleets closed, these big galleasses opened fire. Two Turkish warships sank immediately, but the enemy came on.

Galley warfare during the 16th century was gruesome and unimaginative. Maneuvering was pointless. As quickly as possible, opposing galleys tried to close and ram each other, staving in hulls, smashing oars, and locking themselves together with grappling hooks. Then waves of infantry would swarm over the ramparts to slaughter the enemy and take possession of his ship. Because of the position of the oars, most cannons on galleys were located on the forecastle, the forward battle tower, but more often than not they were loaded with grapeshot and angled back to cover the sides of the ship and fire at the assaulting infantry. This was really a kind of land warfare fought at close quarters on small, rolling, wooden battlefields.

So the battle now developed as the Turks and Christians sailed into each other. As galley smashed into galley with horrendous groans and shudders, soldiers stormed across the decks in fierce hand-to-hand combat. There were volleys of bullets, javelins, catapult stones, and poisoned arrows. Burning pinecones, pitch, and quicklime were thrown onto the enemy's decks. Nails were strewn on the planks to stop boarding parties. Casualties were heavy, the decks ran red with blood, and rarely was mercy shown to the wounded. If a vessel was to burn or sink, the soldiers, crew, and oarsmen were doomed.

The *Marquesa* was in the thick of it. The noise and tumult were overwhelming. Firebrands arched overhead, and smoke enveloped the ship. Cervantes stood in the ranks loading and firing his harquebus, watching Turkish assault parties melt away under the withering fire. The enemy harquebusiers returned fire, and Cervantes was hit three times. Two bullets penetrated his metal breastplate and thick leather doublet and entered his chest. Another shattered his left hand. He fainted and fell to the deck, but came to and rose to his feet once more. The Turks stormed the ship again, and Cervantes had to fight in close quarters with his sword. All was confusion and terror. When the crisis had passed and the *Marquesa* had driven off the enemy, Captain Francisco de Sancto Pietro and 40 others were dead, and more than 100 men were wounded.

In the middle of the channel, in one of those rare confrontations that would have seemed entirely appropriate to medieval knights, the flagship of the Spanish commander, the *Real*, was attacked by the flagship of the Turkish commander, the *Sultana*. Whether Don Juan de Austria actually crossed swords with Ali Pasha is not known, but a savage struggle took place between the soldiers of the two vessels. Other galleys of both fleets came up and joined the fight. Don Juan was wounded in the heel. Finally, Ali Pasha was struck by a bullet and fell. A soldier cut off his head and held it up for the Spaniards to see. The *Sultana* was captured.

Leaderless, the Turkish fleet began to crumble. Many small differences began to have a telling effect. The fire discipline of the Spanish harquebusiers was superior. The Turkish soldiers had no armor and no heavy leather curtains along the sides of their ships to stop arrows. The big Spanish galleasses were unassailable. At the right moment, Don Juan brought up his reserves. The Turkish captains, those that could, began to break off and turn back. The battle turned into a massacre of panic-stricken Turks. By late afternoon, most of the fighting had subsided, and the Spanish could see that they had won a great victory.

The Battle of Lepanto was the greatest and the bloodiest battle ever fought by oared ships, greater than the Battle of Salamis, where the Greeks stopped the Persians in 480 B.C., greater than Actium, where Octavian routed Marc Antony in 31 B.C. When it was over, only about 50 Turkish ships had escaped. More than 100 had been sunk or destroyed, and more than 130 had been captured. Some 30,000 Turks had died, and 7,000 had been taken prisoner. More than 10,000 Christian slaves—oarsmen in the enemy galleys—had been liberated. Insofar as it destroyed the momentum of Turkish westward expansion, it was a victory, and certainly the Spaniards believed that a defeat at Lepanto would have meant the end of Christian Europe.

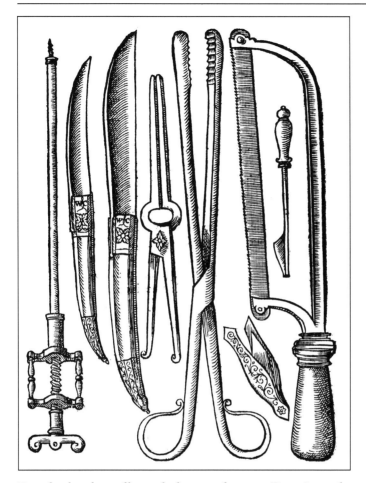

But the battle really ended as a stalemate. Don Juan de Austria had hoped to assault the Turkish garrisons along the Greek coast, to drive back the occupying forces on land, perhaps even to retake the island of Cyprus in the eastern Mediterranean or raid Constantinople itself. But the Christian fleet was spent. Of the 28,000 Spanish infantry who went into battle, more than 7,000 were dead and 15,000 were wounded. There could be no question of continuing the campaign.

In the three weeks it took the fleet to sail back to Messina, Cervantes lay below deck, along with many others, feverish and in pain from his wounds.

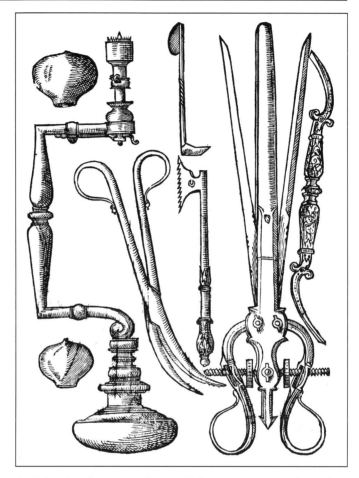

At Messina he was taken off the *Marquesa* and put into a military hospital. Such places could be dangerous.
Doctors had little understanding of the causes or
control of infection. Some of the medical proce-
dures—bleeding, amputation by unsterilized in-
struments—killed more patients than they saved.
Cervantes was lucky, however, and after six months he
was well enough to be discharged. The balls that had
entered his chest had not damaged any vital organs.
But his shattered left hand would not heal, and it
would be useless to him for the rest of his life.

Out of the hospital in April 1572, Cervantes was
able to participate in several more abortive military

adventures, although with his mangled left hand it is unlikely he was any longer a front-line infantryman. Nevertheless, in late summer he was back in the Peloponnisos with a smaller naval force under Marcantonio Colonna. Colonna chased the Turks for a while but could not force them into battle, and the campaign came to nothing.

In early 1573, the Christian alliance broke apart when Venice signed a separate peace treaty with the Ottoman Empire. Philip II was secretly pleased by the betrayal. He had felt all along that military operations against the Turks in the eastern Mediterranean bled the Spanish treasury mainly to protect the commerce of Venice and the other Italian city-states. Now he was free to direct more of his forces against the rebellious Dutch, and to carry out a large-scale punitive expedition against the pirates of North Africa who harassed Spanish shipping in the western Mediterranean.

In October 1573, Cervantes once again found himself under the command of Don Juan de Austria, this time as part of a fleet of 200 vessels and 20,000 soldiers who captured the North African city of Tunis, relieving Spanish troops who had earlier captured the fortress of La Goleta overlooking the city. But now political rivalries intervened. Philip II had simply wanted a destructive raid to render the city unable to support piratical activities, but his commander, Don Juan, had ambitions to build himself a kingdom in Tunis and did not destroy the city. It was to be a disastrous mistake.

After taking Tunis, most of Don Juan's troops, Cervantes included, retired for the winter to the island of Sardinia, about 200 miles to the west of Italy. In September 1574 a refurbished Turkish fleet of 300 vessels and 40,000 soldiers attacked the city of Tunis. Before Don Juan could get a relief force across the

Mediterranean, the fortress of La Goleta was taken, and the city fell to the Turks soon after.

It was all over. Tunis was once again a valuable base of operations for the Turks and the Barbary pirates. Don Juan's dreams of a North African kingdom were shattered. Philip's campaigns in the Mediterranean had cost many lives and drained the Spanish treasury, and accomplished little else. The Turkish threat ceased of its own accord when Selim II suddenly died, and the internal struggle for the succession turned the Ottoman Empire's energies inward.

Cervantes returned with the army to Naples. Except for the summer campaigns in the Mediterranean, he had spent the better part of five years in Italy. Here he had been exposed to Italian Renaissance literature and poetry, and to a freer intellectual climate. He had been befriended by the Duke of Sessa, the governor of Sicily, who kept a salon in Naples where artists and writers would meet. Many of his army friends were poets, and he began to write more poetry, inspired perhaps by an affair with a mysterious Neapolitan beauty named Silena, about whom little is known other than that Cervantes frequently refers to her in his poems. Most of 1575 was a good year for Cervantes, a year of pleasure, passion, and literary pretension.

But it was time to go home. Cervantes was 28 years old and nothing but a common soldier. With his shattered left hand, continued service with the army would be difficult. In any case, by this time he may have become skeptical about the glories of war, having seen so much blood and suffering achieve so little. Literary ambitions were beginning to awaken in him. Others of his generation had found careers for themselves in the Spanish court, its civil bureaucracy, or the Church. He believed that if he wanted to advance himself, he would have to return to Spain.

In September 1575, Miguel and his brother Rodrigo, having secured permission from their commanders, boarded the *Sol* and in the company of three other galleys set out from Naples to return to Spain. A storm separated the *Sol* from her companion vessels, and on the night of September 26, somewhere off the coast of France, Cervantes' ship was attacked and overwhelmed by Barbary pirates. Three Algerian galleys had run the *Sol* down and, after several hours of bloody fighting, had compelled her to surrender. How bitter and ironic it must have seemed, and such a telling comment on the failure of Philip's military policy, to have come all this way to sweep the infidel from the Mediterranean, to have actually beaten him, and now to be his captive.

Unfortunately for Cervantes, his captors discovered in his possession a number of letters of recommendation from the duke of Sessa and Don Juan de Austria himself. These marked him as a man who might command a considerable ransom. The pirates returned to Algiers, where Cervantes was separated from his brother. His hands and feet were shackled, and he was marched through the streets to prison. There he would spend the next five years.

On the surface, prison life in Algiers might not seem so bad. Although the prisoners were locked up at night, during the day they were free to go into the city. This freedom, however, was really a compulsion, because they had to work to survive. All over Algiers, thousands of Christian prisoners of war worked as gardeners, haulers, masons, diggers, garbage collectors, personal servants, and menial laborers. Although out of prison, they still wore chains and special uniforms and were carefully watched by the Muslim population. They were worked hard and were easily recognizable by their thin, undernourished bodies. Children in the streets taunted them and threw stones.

The North African city of Algiers. Soon after his release from the hospital, Cervantes boarded a ship for Spain, where he hoped to focus on his writing. However, on the way his ship was overrun by pirates, and he was captured and brought to Algiers, where he was thrown in jail.

Their masters could beat and even kill them with impunity. Some were tortured and publicly executed. The chopping off of an ear or nose was a common punishment. Others were sold into outright slavery. Still others suffered perhaps the worst fate, to be sent to the galleys and chained to the oars, to row for the enemy until both strength and will gave out. Cervantes was not a candidate for the galleys because of his useless left hand, and because he was thought to be ransomable, he escaped these forms of backbreaking labor.

Cervantes' new master, Dali Mami, commander of the Algerian fleet, set a price of 500 escudos for his release. Cervantes protested that he was a common soldier and worth nothing near that sum. He was put in irons and confined to a dungeon to increase his enthusiasm for raising the money. It instead increased his desire to escape. When he was let out of the dungeon, in late January 1576, he bribed a Moor to act as guide and with eight others quietly went down to the edge of the city one night, and began the trek to Oran, still held by the Spanish, some 200 miles to the west. After a few days their guide deserted them, and they had no choice but to return to Algiers. Cervantes took upon himself all responsibility for the escape attempt and was roughed up and put in irons again.

In March 1576, Gabriel de Casteneda, a fellow prisoner of Cervantes who had fought with him at Lepanto and who had tried to escape with him to Oran, negotiated his ransom and returned to Spain. He carried letters from Cervantes, which he gave to the prisoner's family in Madrid. They began frantic efforts to raise the ransom. They sold their household possessions. An elaborate hoax was devised whereby his father, Rodrigo, pretended to die so that his mother Doña Leonor could better play on the sympathies of the agencies responsible for rescuing captives. The ploy elicited a grant of 60 escudos. Two of Cervantes' sisters, Andrea and Magdalena, had developed into pretty and flirtatious young women, and they were constantly bringing suit against one young man after another for breach of promise—failure to offer marriage after a passionate love affair—and it was hoped that some money could be raised this way.

In late April 1577, a group of Spanish clerics arrived in Algiers to ransom as many prisoners as they could. The matter was becoming touchy, for Sebastian I, the young king of Portugal, had been killed along with 8,000 of his soldiers in an unsuccessful attempt to capture Morocco, and in Algiers animosity toward the Christian slaves increased after this attack. The money pledged for Cervantes was not nearly enough, so by mutual agreement it was all used to ransom his brother. In August, Rodrigo and more than 100 others were freed and sailed for Spain. He had secret instructions from Miguel to hire a frigate and have it return to Algiers in late September.

Cervantes was plotting escape again. He had found a cave along the coast and had induced 14 prominent fellow prisoners to disappear from their places of confinement and hide in the cave to wait for the rescue ship while Cervantes secretly sent them food and supplies every day. They waited in the cave for five months. Rodrigo made the arrangements, and the ship sat off the Algerian coast for two days, but the group was betrayed and recaptured. Cervantes again assumed full responsibility for the escape attempt and was thrown into prison for several months.

He was at it again in late 1578. He paid a Moor to secretly travel to Oran and plead with the Spanish governor-general there, Don Martín de Córdoba, himself once a captive of the Muslims, to come and rescue him. The Moor was discovered and brutally killed. Cervantes managed to escape punishment, but his captor, Dali Mami, sold him to Hassan Pasha, the governor of Algiers, who raised his ransom to 1,000 escudos.

There was a fourth, rather ingenious escape plot in September 1579. Cervantes had befriended a free citizen of Algiers, one Abderrahmen, a Spanish Christian who had converted to the Muslim faith and adopted an Arabic name, but who was now having second thoughts about his conversion and wanted to return to Spain. Cervantes convinced a Valencian merchant who was visiting Algiers to lend Abderrahmen a large sum of money. Abderrahmen was to pretend that he wanted to become a corsair, or Barbary pirate, and buy an armed frigate. This would not have seemed unusual, as many of the sea raiders in the Algerian fleet were Christian renegades. Cervantes and 60 other prisoners would man the ship and escape. With so many people involved, betrayal was almost inevitable. A Christian monk, Juan Blanco de Paz, revealed the scheme to Hassan Pasha, and Cervantes was recaptured. This time he was told he would be hanged. He was led to the gallows, and a noose was placed around his neck. But Pasha, who still hoped for a ransom, had no intention of hanging Cervantes; the entire ordeal was just an attempt to intimidate him. The noose was removed, and Cervantes was thrown back into prison for another five months.

Cervantes was released from prison in the spring of 1580, just before a new group of Spanish clerics, monks of the Trinitarian order, arrived in Algiers to buy the release of more captives. The Trinitarians had with them pledges for all the money that the Cervantes family could raise. Cervantes' father had feigned death a second time—an interesting comment on the efficiency of the Spanish bureaucracy—and the "widow" Doña Leonor had squeezed another 300 escudos out of the Royal Council.

Negotiations dragged on for months. Hassan Pasha would not come down from his demand for 1,000 escudos, but his term as governor of Algiers was coming to an end, and he would soon be returning to Constantinople. Cervantes feared he would be dragged along and lost forever within the capital of the Ottoman Empire. The situation was quite desperate. On September 19, 1580, Cervantes was led down to the docks and marched aboard one of the galleys waiting to take Hassan Pasha home. He was chained to a bench and looked with despair at the oars before him. On deck, Hassan Pasha and a Trinitarian friar, Juan Gil, continued to argue over Cervantes' ransom as the ships made ready to get under way. On a whim, perhaps more to get this pest of a Christian friar out of his hair than anything else, Hassan Pasha reduced the ransom to 500 escudos, but he wanted it all right away, in gold. Not having quite enough cash, the friar ran from the ship into the town to plead with the local moneylenders for a loan, which he was able to secure. He returned with the sum, and Cervantes' chains were cut. With a forlorn look at his friends, whose chains would not be cut and who would row themselves into oblivion, Cervantes leapt from the galley. It had been a remarkable last-minute rescue.

On October 24, 1580, after 10 years away from his native land, 5 of them spent in captivity, a free Miguel de Cervantes boarded a Spanish ship and set out across the Mediterranean for the city of Valencia.

Plaçuela
de
Selenquer

Calle de las Fuentes

Calle de la Priega

Calle de S. Gines

D

CALLE MAI

Plçuela de los Herra de se

de Guadalajara

Calle Nueva

Calle de la Sal

Calle d S

Calle de S. Miguel

PLAÇA MAIOR

23

30

45

PROVIN
ÇIA

M

Plaçuela del C.
de Barajas

T O L E D O

Calle Luperiab

Calle de la Lecruna

Geronima

THE COLLAPSE OF DREAMS

Madrid, Spain. In December 1580, after spending five years in an Algerian prison, Cervantes returned to Madrid, where the following year he landed a job as a diplomatic courier for the king. This enabled him to earn a living while devoting his spare time to writing.

Cervantes and five other ex-prisoners arrived in Valencia on October 30, 1580. On November 1, the city held a festive procession in which the six men were marched through the streets and cheered by the crowds. They were not particularly important as individuals, but the release of captives was always cause for celebration. For the rest of his life, Cervantes would recall the sweetness of his homecoming, and he would always remember the city of Valencia with affection.

There were, however, more important matters to attend to. For example, Cervantes was worried about the 10-year-old warrant for his arrest in the matter of his duel with Antonio de Sigura. He had, quite inadvertently, satisfied the judgment of 10 years' exile, but would the authorities still want to cut off his right hand, now that he had lost the use of his left? He had borrowed money while in captivity and now had debts to pay. He had to capitalize on his service to the king and find a paying position for himself within the royal bureaucracy. Failing that, he was beginning to toy with the idea of earning a living as a man of letters.

For all these reasons he hurried back to Madrid, arriving there on December 15. Once there, he discovered that his family were no longer living together. His brother Rodrigo had reenlisted and was serving in Portugal, which Philip II had annexed after the death of Sebastian I. His two sisters, Andrea and Magdalena, were living elsewhere, presumably with their current lovers. His aging father had sold everything to raise his son's ransom and could no longer support himself. It was a depressing environment, and there was an urgent need for funds, so just a few days after his arrival, Cervantes left for Lisbon, where the king had gone to supervise the integration of Portugal into the Spanish Empire.

In Lisbon he petitioned the king's agents for a veteran's stipend; if not that, then a job. The petition for money was turned down, for as Cervantes was to discover, he was only one of thousands of ex-soldiers hanging about the court expecting to be pensioned off. He was also competing against those families whose sons were still in captivity and desperately needed grants to ransom them. Philip had better uses for his money fighting the Dutch, and there was a new threat from English pirates in the Atlantic. Why waste scarce funds on the wreckage of last year's army? This ingratitude must have burned in the hearts of many veterans.

Cervantes did, however, obtain a temporary assignment as a diplomatic courier. In May 1581, he crossed the Mediterranean again, delivering the king's letters to the governor of Oran, Don Martín de Córdoba, whose help Cervantes had once sought to escape from Algiers. The mission went smoothly, and Cervantes was back in Lisbon in July, once again without funds or employment. In November, he petitioned for a post in the Americas, where it was believed easy fortunes could still be made. The petition was denied.

Cervantes returned to Madrid penniless and for the next two years lived off whatever his mother and sisters could spare for him. He joined a circle of writers, poets, and playwrights, some of them friends from his youth and others he had met in the army. He began to fancy himself a writer. By the summer of 1583, he had completed his first major work, *La Galatea*, a pastoral novel. Such novels were set in idyllic country surroundings and told of the love affairs and intrigues of shepherds and simple country folk, spiced with mistaken identities, revenge killings, and various melodramatic adventures. They were a kind of escapist literature that became popular in Spain as the national economic decline and the pressure of religious orthodoxy turned people away from the material and intellectual severity of their real lives. Although *La Galatea* was not published until 1585, it was widely known and highly regarded among Cervantes' literary friends.

It was also in 1583 that Cervantes' first play was performed, probably on an outdoor stage in one of Madrid's plazas. As he said later with characteristic humor and modesty, between 1583 and 1587 he "composed up to twenty or thirty plays which were all performed without attracting offerings of cucumbers or other missiles." The texts of most of these plays have not survived. Some, like *Life in Algiers* and *The Dungeons of Algiers*, were based on his experiences in captivity. *La batalla naval* recalled the battle of Lepanto. *The Siege of Numantia* was a patriotic epic about a Spanish fortress that for 20 years resisted the conquering Romans, until in 133 B.C., it fell to the legions of Scipio and, as at Masada, its citizens committed suicide rather than surrender. *Numantia* was Cervantes' most ambitious play and the closest to true epic tragedy.

Cervantes enjoyed his modest success as a playwright, but it was hardly a way to make a living. He had also tried for greater realism in his works, setting them in the middle of recent historical events and creating characters based on his broad knowledge of life in the army, in prison, and in the streets of Spanish cities. But this brought him into conflict with the more popular Lope de Vega, whose flamboyant and melodramatic plays were all the rage. Cervantes nursed a grudge that his theater pieces were not better appreciated, and for years both he and Lope, and their respective supporters, carried on a critical war of words against each other.

In 1583 and 1584, Cervantes' romantic life became quite complicated. He took a lover, Ana Franca de Rojas, the wife of a Madrid tavern keeper whose inn was a hangout for actors and theater people. She became pregnant. Then, in September 1584, the poet Pedro Laínez died. Cervantes had known him since their days of soldiering in Naples, and to help Laínez's widow edit and publish her husband's last work, he went to her house in the village of Esquivias, south of Madrid. Here he was a stone's throw away from the plains of southern Castile, southeast of Toledo. Cervantes would come to know and love this region of gently rolling hills covered with vineyards, wheatfields, and windmills, known as La Mancha, where he would eventually set his great masterpiece.

In Esquivias, Cervantes met Doña Catalina de Salazar, the daughter of small landholders in the region. He was 37; she was 20. After knowing each other only three months, they married on December 12, 1584. For reasons that remain unclear, none of the bride's family attended the wedding. Cervantes and Doña Catalina moved into a small two-story house in Esquivias and lived in apparent happiness for several months, with Cervantes commuting into Madrid occasionally to deliver his plays. But then something happened. Cervantes began to spend more and more time away from his new home. An estrangement of

A 16th-century wedding ceremony. Cervantes married Doña Catalina de Salazar on December 12, 1584. However, he proved somewhat unsuited to married life, and within a year the marriage began to break up.

A 16th-century wedding ceremony. Cervantes married Doña Catalina de Salazar on December 12, 1584. However, he proved somewhat unsuited to married life, and within a year the marriage began to break up.

some kind had taken place, and by 1586 Cervantes was for all practical purposes no longer living with his wife.

It is known that shortly after his marriage, Ana, his mistress, gave birth to Isabel, his illegitimate daughter. But it is not known whether or not his wife became aware of his indiscretion at this time, or if she did, whether or not this contributed to their estrangement. In any case, the marriage had clearly failed in less than a year.

Meanwhile, the final act of King Philip's tragedy was about to begin. In 1581, the seven northern provinces of the Netherlands, under the leadership of Prince William of Orange, had declared their independence from Spain. Successive expeditions under Don Juan de Austria—who died in 1578—and the prince of Parma had failed to crush the staunchly Protestant Dutch. Elizabeth I of England had been aiding the new Dutch republic. In 1585, she had gone so far as to send the Earl of Leicester with 6,000 English troops to support William. English and Dutch privateers had been attacking Spanish ports in the Americas and were capturing or destroying the vital treasure galleons. Philip began to see all his troubles as emanating from the English throne, and in 1586 he

ordered that plans be drawn up to build a vast Armada for an invasion of England.

The massive effort to build an invasion fleet could hardly have been kept secret from English spies. When Elizabeth was told of Philip's plans, she reacted swiftly. She executed the imprisoned Queen Mary and about 800 of her followers, ending forever the threat of a Catholic coup d'état. Frantic efforts began to reinforce the English fleet. Elizabeth was not without able and experienced naval commanders, and she now entrusted one of her bravest, Sir Francis Drake, known to the Spanish as El Draque, with a daring raid, as Drake put it, "to singe the beard of the Spanish king."

Showing a level of dash and seamanship that Philip had failed to anticipate, on April 29, 1587, Drake led 26 English ships into the Spanish harbor of Cádiz, where ships of the great Spanish Armada were beginning to assemble. By the time Drake sailed away, with no losses, about 30 Spanish ships had been destroyed.

Preparations for the invasion continued as if nothing had happened. The original plan called for an Armada of 800 ships and 90,000 men. Only about 130 vessels had actually been assembled, and they were mostly of old design and slow. These were not the shallow-draft galleys used in the Mediterranean, but true sailing galleons, though many had oars as well as sails. Supplies were gathered with all the slowness and ineptitude of which the royal bureaucracy was capable, and as Cervantes was to find out personally, in the countryside there was growing resistance to all the exactions and confiscations and recruitment drives. The nation was tired, and only Philip's dreams sustained the drive toward war. He truly believed the English would rise up and depose their Protestant Queen as soon as Spanish troops landed. The man Philip appointed to command the Armada, Alonso Pérez de Guzmán el Bueno, the duke of Medina-Sidonia, tried to turn down the appointment, citing lack of naval experience and a tendency toward seasickness. Philip insisted that he take command. The ill omens were there to be read by anyone who chose to do so.

Cervantes had his hand in these events in a minor and unpleasant way. In Seville in the autumn of 1585, he obtained employment as a commissary for the Spanish navy. He was to travel through the small towns of Andalusia, requisition wheat from local farmers, issue worthless government receipts for what he took, have the wheat milled and baked into biscuits, and then ship the food to ports of embarkation at Cádiz and Lisbon. To ensure collections, he was given the power of search and seizure. He could impose fines and even arrest and imprison people. Traveling through the towns of Écija, La Rambla, Castro de Río, Espejo, and Cabra, Cervantes at first cringed at stealing the harvests of these mostly poor farmers, but under pressure from his superiors he hardened himself and became an efficient, if unpopular, tax collector. He had to deal with local gentry who used every trick in the book to avoid paying their allotments, including going over his head to the king's agents and accusing Cervantes of keeping fraudulent accounts. Twice he inadvertently took wheat from Church lands, and twice he wound up in court fighting the excommunication orders of local clerics.

With Cervantes and hundreds of other commissary agents still collecting provisions, the Armada sailed for England in July 1588. The Spanish fleet consisted of 130 ships, more than 8,000 sailors, and some 20,000 soldiers, one of whom, incidentally, was Cervantes' rival, Lope de Vega, who would survive the battle. Things went wrong from the beginning. The Spanish were unable to rendezvous with the duke of Parma in the Netherlands, whose troops were waiting to be ferried across the English Channel in special barges. The reduced invasion force continued on. The English were waiting for them. An army had been assembled at Tilbury, and signal fires up and down the channel coast would show where the Spanish were amassing.

On July 21, 1588, the Armada arrived off the coast of Plymouth, sailing forward in a huge crescent-shaped formation seven miles wide. The smaller English fleet that came to meet them was commanded by Lord Howard of Effingham in his flagship, *Ark*

Lord Howard of Effingham, the commander of the English fleet that clashed with the Spanish Armada off the coast of Plymouth, England, in July 1588 and forced it into a rapid retreat. The devastating defeat inspired Cervantes to compose two poems marking the event.

Royal. With him were the ablest and bravest of the English sea raiders—Drake, Hawkins, Frobisher, Raleigh—all with vessels that were smaller, faster, and more maneuverable than the Spanish ships. There followed a running sea battle lasting several days in which the Spanish fleet was driven back to the French coast at Calais. There, on the night of July 29, the English set some of their own ships on fire and drove them into the crowded Spanish squadrons, taking a heavy toll.

The Armada was effectively defeated at this point, but that was not the end of the ordeal. Bottled up in the narrow channel between England and France by Howard's fleet, the Spanish could not sail south, the direct route back to Spain. They were forced to sail north all the way around England and down the west coast of Ireland before they could escape. There they were assailed by violent storms that sank and scattered more vessels.

Preparations had been handled so incompetently that on this long, unexpected voyage ships ran out of water and had to contend with rotting food supplies. The Spanish died of hunger and disease, and the Irish coast was said to be littered with their bodies. Only about half the vessels eventually returned to Spain, and the survivors were sickly and beaten.

Because of the long, roundabout, disorganized retreat of the surviving ships, accurate reports of the disaster were slow to reach Spain. Cervantes had time to compose two *Songs to the Invincible Armada*. The first

A map artist's rendition of the 1588 battle between England and Spain. Handily defeated, the Armada retreated to the coast of France but was not allowed to rest there. The English fleet persisted, driving the Spanish north around England and down the west coast of Ireland before they could escape.

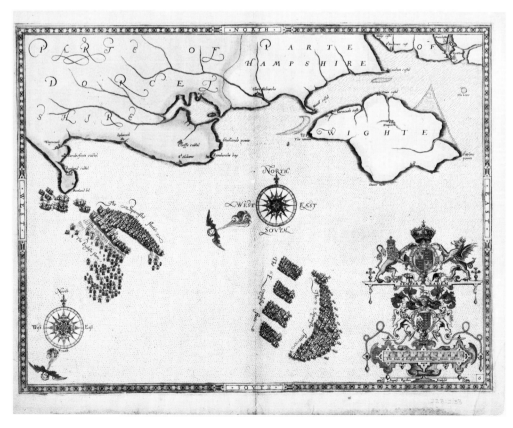

poem merely expresses anxiety over the lack of news; the second recognizes the enormity of the defeat. In the Escorial, however, the truth seemed to have escaped the king's mind. When he learned of the disaster, Philip ordered all the church bells of Spain to be rung in celebration—after all, even a defeat was the will of God. Ignoring the cost, the carnage, and the exhaustion of his country, Philip quietly hoped to raise another invasion fleet and try again at the first opportunity.

Cervantes continued to work, on and off, as a commissary, spending his free time in the streets of Seville, where hard times were swelling the crowds of pícaros to alarming proportions. Crime and lawlessness were common. But Cervantes' meager income forced him into the company of beggars, thieves, pimps, ex-soldiers, dispossessed peasants, gamblers, and assassins. Except for a small aristocracy and the privileged of the Church, most of Spain was being pushed into poverty by its wars. But for Cervantes, the pícaros would become a rich source of characters for his fiction.

In May 1590, Cervantes petitioned the Council of the Indies, again hoping for a position with the colonial administration in the New World. He was turned down. He continued to work as a commissary, but the job was becoming impossible. There was less and less to collect from an increasingly hostile populace. Furthermore, the king had become dissatisfied with the size of the collections and had appointed a special commission to investigate corruption within the commissary system. A number of Cervantes' superiors in the bureaucracy were jailed and hanged, and between 1591 and 1594 he spent a good deal of time in Madrid courts proving that he had not cheated the government. In April 1594, all commissary agents were ordered to suspend their work, and Cervantes was unemployed again. In October 1594, his mother, Doña Leonor, died; his father had died in 1585.

In its final act, the Spanish tragedy almost turned into farce. As Philip planned his next invasion fleet, on June 30, 1596, a small force of English ships under Lord Howard and the earl of Essex again sailed into Cádiz harbor. After sinking more than 50 ships, they debarked an Anglo-Dutch army of 16,000 troops who burned the city. But the greatest injury was that they stayed more than two weeks. With their hard-pressed armies spread throughout Europe, their civil and military administration worn out and corrupt, and their people impoverished and now experiencing pockets of genuine famine, the Spanish could not muster the forces to drive their enemies from one of their own cities. After the raid, Cervantes wrote a

The port of Cádiz. In June 1596, under the command of Sir Francis Drake, a small English fleet entered Cádiz harbor and sank more than 50 Spanish vessels. Some 16,000 English troops moved on the city and drove countless citizens from their homes and businesses.

poem to the Duke of Medina-Sidonia, still commander of Spanish naval forces in spite of the Armada debacle. The poem drips with sarcasm. Cervantes, approaching 50, had few illusions about the destiny of Spain.

How Cervantes supported himself in the years right after his commissary work is unknown. Probably there were small contributions from his sisters, a few friends, even his abandoned wife. He was still living in Seville and exposed to its street life. The festering discontent of the pícaros must have reinforced Cervantes' own experiences. By 17th-century standards, he was beginning to enter old age. He had sacrificed and suffered in the best traditions of knightly honor

A sample from the accounts kept by Cervantes during his tenure as commissary, or tax collector, for the Spanish crown during the late 1500s.

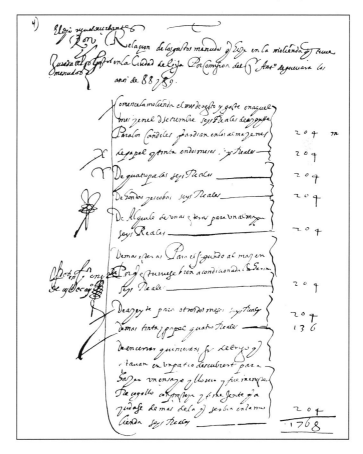

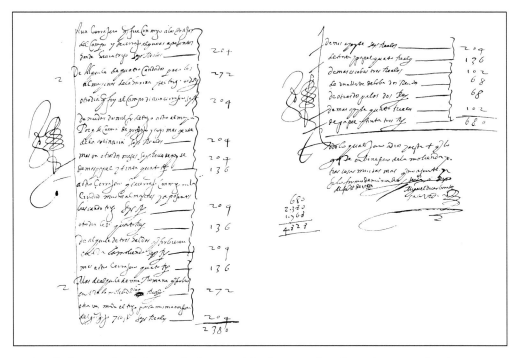

and religious principle, and along with thousands of others of his generation he had not been able to trade that sacrifice for a decent means of livelihood.

It was accountancy that ensnared Cervantes next. The king's auditors were still zealously pursuing the matter of corruption among former commissaries, almost as if they believed they would uncover vast new wealth and solve Spain's problems. Digging through fragmentary records of old accounts, eager to find scapegoats, they accused Cervantes of defrauding the government of a portion of his tax collections. Cervantes was almost certainly innocent. It could hardly be said that he had profited from his position, as many others had. His years as a commissary were some of the poorest of his life. As a tax collector, he had done the king's dirty work and endured the wrath of the people whose goods he took. He had to pay his personal and administrative expenses out of his own pocket and hope that a frequently bankrupt govern-

Cervantes' handwritten accounts from his days as a commissary to the Spanish Armada in Andalusia.

ment would pay its receipts and his wages, which they rarely did promptly and not without shaving something off the amount due. If anyone had squandered or stolen money, it was the royal bureaucracy.

In any case, Cervantes was fed up with the indignities of haggling over taxes and accounts. He had been through so many legal battles over these issues that he just ignored the summons to come to Madrid and explain himself. This infuriated a local magistrate, Gaspar de Vallejo, who, in October 1597, ordered him arrested and confined in the Carcel Real de Sevilla. Cervantes was in prison again.

THE MASTERPIECE

C ervantes was confined within the royal prison, one of several jails within the Carcel Real de Sevilla. It was a strange and horrible place by modern standards. There were about 1,800 prisoners confined here in large cells holding groups of various sizes. There was virtually no privacy. In addition to the prisoners, crowds of lawyers, relatives, and prostitutes filled the courtyards and corridors. There were four taverns within the prison, and gambling, fighting, and thievery were common. The guards could be bought, and in fact if one had the money it was possible to buy one's way out of prison for the day.

Cervantes was no stranger to adversity or to prison life, but it must have hurt to find himself in a Spanish prison as a result of a bureaucratic error. The experience was probably sobering in another respect. The life of the pícaros in the streets of Seville had a certain romantic attraction for Cervantes. They lived by their wits and did not work, and in a bizarre sense they were freer than any other class of Spanish society. But in prison their essential villainy became obvious. By this time, Cervantes was deeply cynical about Spanish society, but he had no wish to end his days as an anonymous no-account. In any event, the matter of the missing tax collections seems to have resolved

Cervantes' celebrated character, the deluded nobleman Don Quixote, brandishes a sword and from his armchair bravely does battle with his many formidable fantasies. Cervantes was released from prison within a year and devoted himself entirely to his writing.

81

itself, and by the spring of 1598, Cervantes was out of jail, with a new resolve to accomplish something. Literature was now his only hope.

Cervantes remained in Seville, but just how he earned his living during this period is a mystery. He was probably beginning to sketch out the plots for *Don Quixote* and some of his short stories. In May 1598, his old mistress, Ana Franca de Rojas, died, and his 14-year-old illegitimate daughter, Isabel, was taken in by her grandparents. In September, Philip II died. He had ruled Spain for more than 40 years and brought it to the brink of ruin. Even his grand funeral became something of a farce. In the church, a dispute broke out between a member of the royal court and members of the Inquisition over the seating arrangements. On the spot, the Inquisitors excommunicated the offending courtier, and the entire ceremony had to be postponed until tempers cooled. When the ceremony finally did take place, Cervantes was in the church and read aloud a flattering sonnet that he had written.

In March 1599 the first part of Mateo Alemán's *Guzmán de Alfarache* was published. This bitter picaresque account of a former galley slave who lives by his wits and scoffs at all the grand ideals of imperial Spain was immensely popular. Unlike Alemán, Cervantes had a view of the decay around him that was tempered by a sense of humor, a compassion for people, and a more moderate, humanistic Catholicism that proved more resilient under the pressure of events. Yet he saw in Alemán's novel, with its colorful characters and numerous adventures, a form that he could borrow to tell a much grander tale.

Another tragedy was about to strike Spain, in part the result of drought, bad harvests, bad policy, widespread poverty, and famine. From 1599 to 1601 there was a resurgence of the Black Death, the bubonic

The Spanish writer Mateo Alemán. Alemán's enormously popular picaresque novel, Guzmán de Alfarache, *published in 1599, inspired Cervantes to write a work that was similar in that it presented an array of colorful characters in a series of misadventures.*

plague that people caught from the fleas found on rats and other animals. Within three years it would kill more than 600,000 Spaniards. For the survivors, it was one more blow to the cohesiveness of Spanish society. The disease attacked mainly the poor crowded into the cities. The aristocracy retreated to their estates in the countryside and locked themselves in. Many priests and doctors refused to attend to the sick and dying and tried to save themselves. Class antagonisms were growing.

Where Cervantes spent his time during the plague years is uncertain because records are fragmentary. There is evidence of a reconciliation with his wife, Doña Catalina, and from 1601 to 1602 he may have retreated to the village of Esquivias, living quietly and working on *Don Quixote*.

The new king, Philip III, 20 years old when he assumed the throne, was as rigid and intolerant as his father, but he was also lazy, sickly, and uninterested in the problems of government. He appointed Don Francisco Gómez de Sandoval y Rojas, the duke of Lerma, to manage state affairs while he surrendered himself to lavish entertainments. Under Philip III's reign, French workers, farmers, and craftsmen immigrated to Spain in great numbers to fill up the labor shortage created by the plague. The Spanish army degenerated into an army for hire, so desperate was the monarchy for cash. Later, in 1609, Philip III would finally expel all the Moriscos, the converted Muslims, from Spain. Because of their key positions in certain trades and crafts, their expulsion would only further weaken the Spanish economy. The foreign wars would continue as well. In July 1600, Cervantes would learn that his brother Rodrigo had been killed in the Battle of Nieuwpoort in Flanders.

The duke of Lerma ran the government as he pleased, enriching himself and appointing his relatives to high positions. In 1601, in exchange for a large bribe paid to him by the northern city of Valladolid, he convinced Philip to make it the new capital and to move there. A vast army of officials, bureaucrats, and noble families moved with him, leaving Madrid deserted. Cervantes' sisters, Andrea and Magdalena, had been supporting themselves as seamstresses and needed the business of these wealthy families, so in 1603 they packed up and followed the crowd to Valladolid. Cervantes arrived there with Doña Catalina in 1604, and the whole family, along with other cousins and relatives, lived together in relative harmony in a complex of apartments on the Calle de Rastro in a slum neighborhood. Even Cervantes' illegitimate daughter, Isabel, had been taken in as a servant for Magdalena.

In January 1605 about 750 copies of a cheap, error-filled, paperbound edition of Part I of *Don Quixote* appeared for sale in the Madrid and Valladolid bookshops of Francisco de Robles. Against almost everyone's expectations, the book was an instant success. In fact, it would eventually become a best-seller

The title page of the first edition of Cervantes' Don Quixote, *published in Madrid in 1605. Upon publication, about 750 paperbound copies of the novel were displayed for sale in Madrid and Valladolid; some 400 copies were shipped to the Spanish colonies in America.*

throughout the world, second in sales only to the Bible. Parts of it were known to Cervantes' writer friends before publication. They would have recognized its roots in the romances of chivalry and the picaresque tradition, but they must also have sensed that something revolutionary had happened.

Why has *Don Quixote* been so highly regarded by generation after generation of readers? With, admittedly, some injustice to others who made their contributions, it may be said that Cervantes invented the modern novel.

The novel is distinguished, first of all, in that it is written in prose and not poetry. This was not the case with earlier novels. Even Cervantes' earlier novel *La Galatea*, was written mostly in verse, with occasional prose passages. By abandoning the highly formal, declamatory style and the strict meter and rhyme schemes of poetry in favor of the more relaxed expression of prose sentences, the novel suddenly became capable of a fuller and freer exploration of human experience and the development of human character over time. Speech and conversation in particular became more natural and realistic.

That human character would be the central focus of the novel was an idea introduced into art by the Renaissance period. In the modern novel, in many cases character drives plot. In earlier literature, character might be subordinate to the author's grand design, which might have been the need to teach a moral lesson, to reaffirm a religious doctrine, to put forward a view of history, or to celebrate heroic or legendary events. To the extent that they had to fit into the grand design, characters were flat, and their behavior was unnatural and stereotyped. With Cervantes, events are driven by the actions of unique individuals, a principle that led to greater realism in storytelling. Cervantes revolutionized the novel in the same way

Don Quixote and his sidekick, Sancho Panza, set out on their chivalric mission to slay the agents of evil and right the world's wrongs. Fleshy, pragmatic, and illiterate, Panza is the opposite of his spindly master, who is idealistic and steeped in literary romances.

that his contemporary in England, William Shakespeare, revolutionized drama. The new focus on individual psychology would sustain four centuries of novelists, including Fielding, Dickens, Melville, Flaubert, Balzac, Tolstoy, Dostoyevsky, Conrad, Joyce, and others.

The hero of *Don Quixote* is Alonso Quixada, or Quexana, an undistinguished hidalgo, a poor gentleman from La Mancha earning a meager living as the landlord of some small country properties. His one passion is his obsessive reading of the romances of chivalry, the popular stories of Lancelot, Roland, El Cid, and other famous knights who led adventurous lives rescuing maidens, battling the forces of evil, seeking justice, and righting wrongs wherever they went. All this reading unhinges Quixada's mind, and he decides to become such a knight himself and venture forth to do good deeds, to recreate the Golden Age out of this "age of iron." The tall, gaunt, spindly-legged old man dons an old suit of armor and renames himself Don Quixote de la Mancha. He takes an undernourished farm horse for his mount and names it Rocinante (from the Spanish *rocin*, or "nag"). As all knights must have a lady to champion, he chooses a plain peasant girl from a nearby village and renames her Dulcinea del Toboso.

As Don Quixote sets out on his first adventures, it becomes clear that he is truly mad and cannot correctly interpret the reality around him. He lives in a world of chivalric fantasy while the reality he does not see is continually undermining and defeating his efforts to

In perhaps the most well known scene in Don Quixote, *the protagonist and his mount, Rocinante, are sent flying in a joust with a hostile windmill, which Quixote believes to be an evil giant.*

do good deeds. He comes to an inn, which he is convinced is a castle. Seeing him as just a foolish old man in his clunky armor, the innkeeper and some prostitutes hold a mock ceremony and formally dub him a knight. Leaving the "castle," Quixote next comes upon a farmer beating a young boy tied to a tree. He forces the farmer to free the boy and exacts his promise to pay the boy his back wages. As soon as Quixote is gone, of course, the farmer, who cares not for knightly oaths, resumes his whipping. Quixote next encounters a group of silk merchants on the road, and blocking their path, he demands that they attest to the beauty of his lady Dulcinea. The hard-nosed merchants refuse without seeing a likeness of her. The insulted Quixote charges into them, and as will happen time and again, he is pummeled and left lying in the road, senseless, his lance broken. A neighbor slings him over Rocinante's back and leads him home.

While Quixote recuperates, his best friends, the local priest and barber, conduct a parody of the Inquisition by burning most of the books in his library to prevent him from filling his head with more silly adventures. They fail, of course, and Quixote is soon off again. This time he takes with him a squire, a fat little peasant named Sancho Panza (*panza* in Spanish means "potbelly"). Sancho is everything Don Quixote is not—pragmatic rather than idealistic, concerned with matters of the flesh rather than of the spirit. Illiterate, he has never read a romance of chivalry. He will give his master the name that so many readers have believed describes Cervantes himself— the Knight of the Mournful Countenance.

Quixote's new adventures reveal new heights of self-delusion. In a scene as well known as any in world literature, the mad knight perceives a windmill to be an evil giant and charges at it. Ensnared by one of the windmill's vanes, he is lifted from his horse and

Sancho Panza, over-whelmed at the recognition of his own simple nature, embraces his mule in a scene from Don Quixote. *In the course of the novel, Panza is awarded the governorship of a small village, grows disenchanted with the life of a noble-man, and quits to return happily to his peasant roots.*

thrown crashing to the ground. From this scene, the phrase "tilting at windmills" has entered many languages as a common expression for the pursuit of a foolish or hopeless cause. There follows an encounter with a gentleman whose lady Don Quixote believes is being taken somewhere against her will, and this ends in another fight. Don Quixote and Sancho Panza come upon another inn, a "castle" where, in the darkness of night, a serving woman on her way to a rendezvous with her lover stumbles into the knight's arms. Quixote thinks she is the nobleman's—or inn-keeper's—daughter, with whom he has become in-fatuated. Mistaken identities and groping in the dark lead to a huge brawl.

Don Quixote next charges into two flocks of sheep, believing them to be two large armies, Christian and infidel, about to clash. Enraged shepherds loose their slingshots at him, and again Quixote is knocked from his horse. On another occasion, he mistakes an evening funeral procession for the entourage of a knight he wishes to challenge, and he scatters the frightened priests conveying the body. One night, the knight and his squire hear the loud pounding of fulling mills, which used heavy weights to thicken and strengthen woolen fabrics. The hellish noise convinces Don Quixote that evil forces are nearby, and he girds himself for battle. When the cause of the noise is discovered and Sancho begins to laugh, Don Quixote beats him for puncturing the illusion.

Again, a barber's basin, worn on its owner's head to ward off the rain, becomes for Don Quixote an enchanted helmet that he must have. Encountering a group of chained convicts being led to servitude in the galleys, Don Quixote assumes that they are innocent men and attacks their guards. The freed but ungrateful prisoners then pummel him with stones until he falls from his horse, his enchanted helmet shattered. After more adventures, the knight's friends manage to convince him that he has been bewitched and lock him into a wooden cage and drag him home in an ox cart. Thus ends Part I.

It is difficult in a brief space to describe all the elements at work in Cervantes' story. It is, first of all, a crowded mural of colorful 17th-century Spanish characters—peasants, innkeepers, merchants, prostitutes, priests, rogues, soldiers—all struggling to survive in a squalid landscape that is a parody of the Golden Age. It is full of topical allusions, that is, references to people, places, and events known to the author and his readers, that poke fun at the Crown, the Church, the Inquisition, and contemporary personalities. There is also the central conflict between illusion and reality, between the mad visions of Don Quixote and the cynical pragmatism of nearly everyone else, which continuously confronts the reader with the enormous gap between the dreams and pretensions of imperial Spain and the miserable lives of its people. All the beatings and pummelings received by Don Quixote and Sancho Panza in their efforts to do good convey a sense of foolish adventurism and farcical defeat that would have been instantly recognizable to any 17th-century Spaniard. But it is not an angry novel, as was Mateo Alemán's *Guzmán de Alfarache*. Cervantes approached his world with compassion, affection, and humor. Many of the scenes he created are utterly hilarious. This is not only a great novel, but a great *comic* novel. More than anything else, *Don Quixote* is a pleasure to read.

The second part of *Don Quixote* was not published until 1615, 10 years after the first part appeared. In the interim, the first part had established Cervantes' reputation as a writer and had endeared the characters of the mad knight and his squire to thousands of Spaniards. The ever-inventive Cervantes turned even his own success into literary material. The second part of the novel begins with the arrival in Don Quixote's village of a young scholar, Sanson Carrasco, who informs Don Quixote and Sancho Panza that someone has written a book about their adventures. Don Quixote wishes to know which of his exploits are the most popular and why. A general discussion of literature and literary tastes follows, and the novel *Don Quixote* is criticized by its main character.

Also, in 1614, just a year before the publication of Part II, a "false" *Don Quixote* appeared, the work of an unknown author who signed himself Alonso Fernández de Avellaneda. Whoever he was, he was probably a literary ally of Cervantes' old nemesis, Lope de Vega, for he openly ridiculed Cervantes and the style of the first part. Constructed as a sequel, the counterfeit *Quixote* was a pale imitation of the real thing, and in Part II Cervantes absorbed one of Avellaneda's characters into his own story, making the character swear that the first book he appeared in was not nearly as good as this one. Such gamesmanship and literary pranksterism seem to have been common in the early experiments with the novel and can also be found in the works of the English writers Henry Fielding and Lawrence Sterne. Cervantes was acutely aware of himself as a literary experimenter, and literary criticism and self-criticism occur throughout the novel—as with his social criticism, often in disguised or symbolic form. There is even an elaborate fabrication concerning who the real author of *Don Quixote* is. Cervantes claims merely to have discovered the manuscript of an Arab historian, Cide Hamete Benengeli. When, in Part II, Don Quixote learns that his story is being told by an infidel, he is deeply disturbed.

The 10 years between the first and second parts of *Don Quixote* also produced a more mature and seasoned writer. The comic hijinks of Part I continue in Part II, but they are subdued, and Cervantes seems more interested in deeper issues, such as the psychological relationship and growing friendship between Don Quixote and Sancho Panza. Roles become blurred as Sancho seems to take more seriously the illusory causes of his master and to develop a stronger protective instinct toward him, while Don Quixote's madness becomes more questionable. In Part II, Don Quixote is subjected to the imaginative fantasies of other people, who know his weaknesses from Part I and seek to manipulate him. He is no longer the sole author of these fantasies. He loses control of them and is confused by them. This leads to moments of self-analysis and genuine insight during which Don Quixote seems to retreat from total immersion in unreality.

Much of Part II revolves around the "lady" Dulcinea and how Don Quixote will cope with this fantasy creation. Early on, Don Quixote and Sancho discuss returning to the village of El Toboso to see her. But it is a trip they cannot make, because Dulcinea is really an illiterate peasant girl named Aldonza Lorenzo. To confront her in person would shatter the knight's illusions. Both the knight and his squire seem to recognize this, and they create an elaborate subterfuge to avoid making the trip. But illusion still dominates. When Don Quixote attends a puppet show, he is so moved by the plight of the heroine puppet that he jumps up and tries to hack the villain puppet to pieces, destroying the whole puppet show in the process.

After more adventures, Don Quixote and Sancho come to a real castle and are taken in by a real duke and duchess. Cervantes creates an ironic contrast between the idealism and nobility of his hero, a false aristocrat, and the lethargy and moral weakness of the true Spanish aristocrats. The duke and duchess happen to have read Part I of the novel and decide to subject the hero to a number of cruel hoaxes to test his madness and his faithfulness to Dulcinea. There are bizarre stagings of medieval fantasies. A young lady of the duchess's retinue is ordered to seduce Don Quixote, but instead she falls in love with him, and the knight's refusal to be seduced creates an awkward scene involving everyone. Before the knight leaves, the duke convinces him that Dulcinea has been enchanted and that the spell can only be broken if Sancho subjects himself to 3,000 lashes of the whip. In a state of confusion, Don Quixote broods about whether to inflict this punishment on someone he has grown to love.

On the road again, Don Quixote again meets the young scholar Sanson Carrasco, this time outfitted in full armor and disguised as a knight himself. After a brief combat, Don Quixote is unhorsed and defeated, and Carrasco extracts a promise from him to go home and cease his chivalric adventures for at least a year. This Don Quixote must do on his honor as a knight, but he decides to spend the year living out another fantasy from a different literary tradition. He and Sancho will become shepherds and live the pastoral life.

There is, however, the spell that Don Quixote believes to have been cast on Dulcinea. He argues with Sancho and insists that the squire endure 3,000 self-inflicted lashes for his lady's sake. Sancho balks until Don Quixote offers to pay him to endure the punishment. The pragmatic Sancho, however, simply walks out of sight and starts to whip the trees. Hearing the noise of the "beating," Don Quixote, confused and worn out by an endless assault of real and illusory events, finds that he must choose between his love for the mythical Dulcinea and his affection for his squire. He calls out for Sancho to stop beating himself.

Don Quixote returns home, where his niece and his housekeeper take him in and scold him like a

Don Quixote rides across the Spanish landscape with numerous figments of his imagination looming behind him. The success of Don Quixote *brought Cervantes some fame but not much money; well into his fifties he continued to live in a Valladolid slum on the meager income he earned from his writing.*

wayward schoolchild. He goes to sleep, and when he wakes up he no longer believes himself to be a knight, but an ordinary country gentleman named Alsonso Quijano de Bueno, who soon dies a peaceful and contented death in bed. Comedy has turned to tragedy. In death, Don Quixote is ennobled. He may have been a mad fool, but his spiritual metal had not tarnished and corroded, as had that of the world around him.

The first part of *Don Quixote* went through many editions in many languages while the author was still alive. It was popular throughout Europe and even in Spain's American colonies. Tall, skinny men were sometimes called Don Quixotes and short, squat ones Sancho Panzas. Cervantes became a minor celebrity, occasionally recognized in public, sometimes called upon to provide a short laudatory poem for important public events.

Cervantes did not earn a great deal of money from the book, however. He continued to live in a Valladolid slum, getting by on leftovers from his sisters' sewing money and the meager earnings from his writing. Cervantes was 58 years old when Part I was published. His life had been hard, sometimes bitter, sometimes cruel, but he now had his measure of literary fame as well as a passionate Christian belief in a better life to come.

Granada, Spain, until the 1570 Morisco rebellion a center for Moorish culture. In 1609, Philip III launched a campaign to expel the Moriscos, on the grounds that they engaged in Muslim practices, which were banned in Spain in 1567.

ONE FOOT IN THE STIRRUP

It began sometime in the late 1590s with intermittent dizzy spells, a strange weakness that neither eating nor sleeping could dispel, and a desperate thirst that no amount of drinking could quench. The disease was known to the ancient Greeks, who called it diabetes, but 17th-century doctors had no remedy. They could, however, predict the disease's course, and Cervantes would have been aware of what he had to look forward to—increasing weakness, a slow wasting away, and if he lived long enough other complications such as loss of eyesight, heart disease, and circulatory problems. The end was always the same, an uncomfortable death. From now on, Cervantes would feel the end slowly approaching every day, and he would struggle toward it with much suffering and little hope.

Spain's great struggle to dominate Europe was also beginning to wind down. In the summer of 1605, Lord Howard of Effingham, now the earl of Nottingham, arrived from England with 500 noblemen to ratify a peace treaty between Spain and England, and there were lavish celebrations in the capital. Cervantes' participation in the festivities may have been cut short. In late June, a certain Don Gaspar de Espeleta was stabbed in the street just a few doors from where Cervantes' clan lived. He died two days later. Though there does not appear to be any evidence of his involvement, Cervantes was questioned and arrested. He was released after one day, and the case against him was dropped a few weeks later, but understandably his distaste for these injustices must have been very strong, and he seems to have left Valladolid to return to Madrid. The royal court followed him in January 1606, when Philip III decided to move the capital back to Madrid. Once again, a massive exodus took place from the old capital to the new, with Cervantes' sisters following the nobility to Madrid to maintain their income as seamstresses.

In 1609, the expulsion of the Moriscos began. The roads were choked with Moorish people moving to

A woman in a traditional Moorish cloak. So many Moriscos were textile workers that the systematic expulsion of them during the early 1600s resulted in a sudden degeneration of Spain's cotton and silk industries and a significant blow to Spain's already struggling economy.

the port cities, from which they scattered themselves throughout Europe and North Africa. Their lands and property were confiscated. On the road, Christian fanatics harassed them. More than a quarter million people were driven out of Spain in one of the Empire's most shameful and self-destructive acts.

For several years, no new works by Cervantes were published, but he was doing a lot of writing, and these were very productive years for him in spite of bad health. He was pushing several different works to completion at the same time, and they would all be finished in a rush in his last years. In April 1609, he joined the Congregation of Unworthy Slaves of the Most Holy Sacrament, a lay group run by the Trinitarian friars. It committed him to sexual abstinence and certain daily religious duties. Clearly, Cervantes was feeling his strength ebb and was making preparations for the next life. On October 9, 1609, his sister Andrea died. His other sister, Magdalena, would pass away two years later. There was some unpleasantness with his illegitimate daughter, Isabel, who had grown into a defiant young woman. She took a lover of whom Cervantes did not approve and gave birth to a daughter who died in 1610. Cervantes and Isabel became estranged, and Cervantes wrote her out of his will, though he had nothing of material value to leave her anyway.

It was customary in these times for a writer to look for a patron, a wealthy aristocrat who would be flattered to have works of literature dedicated to him and who might even respond with a cash donation to keep a hungry writer alive. Cervantes had been cultivating Don Pedro Fernández de Castro y Andrade, the count of Lemos. In 1610, the count had been appointed governor of Naples, and Cervantes hoped to go to Italy with Lemos and become part of his salon of writers and artists. But Cervantes was not chosen.

Don Pedro Fernández de Castro y Andrade, the count of Lemos. Cervantes cultivated a relationship with Lemos in 1610 with the hope of joining him in Italy as a member of his salon of writers and artists, but his scheme failed. In ironic gratitude, Cervantes dedicated several of his works to Lemos.

*The title page of
Cervantes'* Exemplary
Stories *published in
August 1613. An im-
portant theme that runs
through the stories in
this collection is the
redemptive power of
love and the great virtue
in individual sacrifice as
a means to its attain-
ment.*

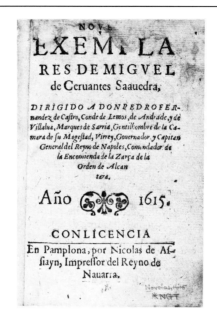

How seriously he was hurt by this, on top of all his other disappointments, is hard to determine, but from this point on all of Cervantes' writings, including Part II of *Don Quixote*, were dedicated to the count of Lemos, perhaps with a good deal of sarcasm.

In August 1613 a new work by Cervantes finally appeared, a collection titled *Exemplary Stories*, which like *Don Quixote* dealt with the corruption of the world and the correct moral response to that corruption. He also infused his characters with greater psychological realism and placed them in the real settings of everyday life. If it is unfair to say that Cervantes invented the modern short story, it can certainly be said that he helped it on its way. The stories were well received by contemporary readers.

In October 1614, Avellaneda's fake *Quixote* appeared. It never presented a serious challenge to Cervantes' literary reputation, but it caused him enough irritation to write into the real Part II numerous insults and criticisms of its author's style. Cervantes felt himself to be an outcast in a world where writers and poets fought for recognition and patronage like a pack of dogs fighting over bones, and he had usually been the loser. Cervantes had long harbored feelings that his poetry and plays in particular and his skills as a writer in general were never properly appreciated by the most vocal Spanish writers and critics. His next work would address this problem directly.

In November 1614, Cervantes published a long, peculiar poem entitled *Voyage to Parnassus*. It was a satirical allegory in which the author makes an imaginary journey to Parnassus, the home of the Muses, the goddesses who inspire poetry. The mountain is being assaulted by thousands of "puny, foolish poets," and Cervantes is called in to help repel the assault. The whole poem was a marvelous opportunity to pass judgement on all his contemporaries, whom he grouped into two armies of good and bad poets.

In early 1615, Cervantes issued a collection of *Eight Plays and Eight Interludes, New and Never Performed*. In the years following the publication of Part I of *Don Quixote*, Cervantes had written a number of plays, but he was unsuccessful in selling them to the acting companies. This time he tried to reach the public directly. Though Cervantes' characterizations were naturalistic and far ahead of those of his contemporaries, his plots were awkward and dull, and it is understandable that the plays were not performed. As a prose novelist, Cervantes would achieve lasting fame, and his literary innovations put virtually everyone else in the camp of the old guard, but he could never quite accept that he was only a second-rate playwright.

In November 1615 the eagerly awaited Part II of *Don Quixote* appeared in the bookshops. Cervantes' first major work, *The Labors of Persiles and Sigismunda*, was finished in March 1616, although it would not be published until after his death.

For his last major piece of writing, Cervantes abandoned his innovative style, his exploration of realism and psychological truth, and his impish sense of humor. He borrowed a story line from the 3rd-century Greek writer Heliodorus and turned it into a standard, morally correct, medieval romantic adventure. Persiles and Sigismunda are in love, but feel that they have sinned by lusting after each other. Seeking redemption, they assume false names and run away to Rome. After a series of incredible adventures that test their love and their faith, they complete their journey and live happily ever after. Although well written, the tone of the novel is melodramatic, its characters flat, and the whole thing rather uninteresting to modern readers. Cervantes' reasons for writing, at this point in his life, a work that so clearly seems to be a step backward remain a mystery.

It is possible that this last work was simply the product of a writer whose powers were waning, for there was little time left for Cervantes. Living in Madrid with his wife in a small ground-floor apartment on what is now called the Calle de Cervantes, the old soldier could feel the wasting away of his body and was probably spending a good deal of time in bed at that point. His parents and sisters were dead; his brother had died in the foreign wars, and he was no longer on speaking terms with his only daughter. In early April 1616, he joined the Order of Saint Francis. The Trinitarian order he already belonged to had become too secular for his taste. On Monday, April 18, he received his last rites from a local priest. During the next two days, he wrote out a dedication and prologue to *Persiles and Sigismunda* in which he borrowed a phrase from an old Spanish ballad and talked about having "one foot already in the stirrup." He wrote to his readers, "My life is drawing to a close, and at the rate my pulse is going it will end its career, at the latest, next Sunday, and that will be the end of me."

His prediction was off by only a day. Not on Sunday but on Saturday, April 23, 1616, Miguel de Cervantes, 69 years old, sank into a coma and died.

The funeral and burial went unrecorded and were certainly not elaborate. Cervantes had led, for the most part, a life of hardship and disappointment, tempered by a small measure of recognition from his contemporaries. He would never know or profit from the worldwide acclaim *Don Quixote* would receive. Not only his life but his whole world and its values had collapsed around him. But he harbored no bitterness. Even at the end, good humor, faith, and charity won out. "Good-by, thanks; good-by, compliments; good-by, merry friends. I am dying, and my wish is that I may see you all soon again, happy in the life to come."

Cervantes published several works during the last decade of his life, but his greatest accomplishment remained Don Quixote. *The author of the world's all-time best-selling work of fiction received little reward for writing it; still, he was not bitter. He bid the world a merry farewell on April 23, 1616.*

CHRONOLOGY

1547   Miguel de Cervantes Saavedra born in Alcalá de
        Henares, Spain

1551   Cervantes family moves to Valladolid

1553   Cervantes family moves to Córdoba

1556   Abdication of Spain's king Charles I, who is
        succeeded by his son, Philip II

1564   Cervantes family moves to Seville

1566   Philip II makes Madrid the capital of Spain, and
        the Cervantes family moves there; anti-Catholic
        mobs attack the churches of the Spanish
        Netherlands; Selim II accedes to the throne
        of the Ottoman Empire

1569   Cervantes leaves Spain for Italy

1571   Goes to Naples and enlists in the Spanish infantry
        assembling there to repel the Turks in the eastern
        Mediterranean; on October 7, Spanish and Italian
        naval forces defeat the Turks at the Battle of
        Lepanto, where Cervantes is wounded

1573   Participates in the military expedition to recapture
        Tunis on the coast of North Africa

1575	While attempting to return to Spain, is captured by Barbary pirates and imprisoned in Algiers along with his brother Rodrigo
1580	Released from prison, Cervantes returns to Valencia; Philip II annexes Portugal
1581	Northern provinces of the Netherlands declare their independence from Spain; war begins between the Spanish and the Dutch, who fight with the support of England
1582	Cervantes' liaison with Ana Franca de Rojas produces an illegitimate daughter, Isabel
1583	Cervantes' first play is produced in Madrid
1584	Cervantes marries Doña Catalina de Salazar
1585	Publishes pastoral novel, *La Galatea*; works as a commissary, raising provisions for the Spanish navy
1587	Sir Francis Drake raids the Spanish port of Cádiz
1588	Defeat of the Spanish Armada
1590	Cervantes' request for a post in the Spanish Americas is denied
1592	Cervantes is arrested and held in prison for allegedly arranging an illegal sale of wheat
1596	The English again raid the port of Cádiz
1597	Philip II's government is bankrupt; accused of cheating the government, Cervantes is arrested and briefly thrown into prison; develops diabetes.

1598	Philip II dies; Philip III accedes to the Spanish throne
1599	*Guzmán de Alfarache*, by Mateo Alemán, is published; new outbreak of plague kills more than a half million Spaniards; Cervantes and his wife move to Esquivias
1600	Cervantes' brother Rodrigo is killed fighting the Dutch in Flanders
1601	Philip III moves the capital to Valladolid, and Cervantes moves there with his wife
1603	James I succeeds England's queen Elizabeth I
1605	Part I of *Don Quixote* published; English and Spanish forces conclude a peace, but war with the Netherlands continues
1606	Spanish capital is moved back to Madrid
1609	Moors are expelled from Spain
1611	King James Version of the Bible is completed
1613	Cervantes' *Exemplary Stories* published
1614	Cervantes publishes *Voyage to Parnassus*; the "false" *Don Quixote* appears
1615	Part II of *Don Quixote* is published
1616	On April 23, Cervantes dies peacefully in bed, shortly after finishing *The Labors of Persiles and Sigismunda*

FURTHER READING

Arbó, Sebastian Juan. *Cervantes: The Man and His Time.* Translated by Ilsa Barea. New York: Vanguard Press, 1955.

Bell, Aubrey Fitz Gerald. *Cervantes.* Norman: University of Oklahoma Press, 1947.

Benardete, Mair José. *The Anatomy of Don Quixote.* Port Washington, NY: Kennikat Press, 1969.

Bergin, Thomas G., and Arnoldo Mondadori Editore. *Cervantes: His Life, His Work, His Times.* New York: American Heritage Press, 1970.

Bloom, Harold, ed. *Miguel de Cervantes.* New York: Chelsea House, 1987.

Byron, William. *Cervantes: A Biography.* New York: Doubleday, 1978.

Cervantes, Miguel. *The Portable Cervantes.* Translated and edited by Samuel Putnam. New York: Viking, 1951.

Church, Margaret. *Don Quixote: The Knight of La Mancha.* New York: New York University Press, 1971.

Crow, John A. *Spain: The Root and the Flower.* Berkeley: University of California Press, 1963.

McKendrick, Melveena. *Cervantes.* Boston: Little, Brown, 1980.

Navarro y Ledesma, Francisco. *Cervantes: The Man and the Genius.* Translated by Don and Gabriela Bless. New York: Charterhouse, 1973.

Predmore, Richard Lionel. *The World of Don Quixote.* Cambridge: Harvard University Press, 1967.

————. *Cervantes.* New York: Dodd, Mead, 1973.

Riley, Edward Calverley. *Cervantes' Theory of the Novel.* Oxford: Clarendon Press, 1962.

Index

JAKE GOLDBERG is an editor and freelance writer based in New York City. He is the author of several books for junior readers and young adults, including a biography of Rachel Carson.

RODOLFO CARDONA is professor of Spanish and comparative literature at Boston University. A renowned scholar, he has written many works of criticism, including *Ramón, a Study of Gómez de la Serna and His Works* and *Visión del esperpento: Teoría y práctica del esperpento en Valle-Inclán.* Born in San José, Costa Rica, he earned his B.A. and M.A. from Louisiana State University and received a Ph.D. from the University of Washington. He has taught at Case Western Reserve University, the University of Pittsburgh, the University of Texas at Austin, the University of New Mexico, and Harvard University.

JAMES COCKCROFT is currently a visiting professor of Latin American and Caribbean studies at the State University of New York at Albany. A three-time Fulbright scholar, he earned a Ph.D. from Stanford University and has taught at the University of Massachusetts, the University of Vermont, and the University of Connecticut. He is the author or coauthor of numerous books on Latin American subjects, including *Neighbors in Turmoil: Latin America*, *The Hispanic Experience in the United States: Contemporary Issues and Perspectives*, and *Outlaws in the Promised Land: Mexican Immigrant Workers and America's Future.*